CHURCHILL COLLEGE CAMBRIDGE
THE GUIDE

'*Felix qui potuit rerum cognoscere causas*. These words from Lucretius were inscribed above the gateway of my college in Cambridge. "Happy the man who knows the causes (the origins) of things." It was the motto for a scientific community – Churchill College was a modern foundation, which contained by statute a minimum of 70 per cent science undergraduates, and its culture was open-minded, democratic, iconoclastic to a degree. I breathed in a pioneering atmosphere of excitement and questioning.'

Richard Holmes, FBA, OBE
(undergraduate in English, 1964-7)
Sidetracks (London, 2000), p. 369

Published by Churchill College

Published by Churchill College, Cambridge © 2009

ISBN: 978-0-9563917-1-1

Not to be reproduced or transmitted in any form without permission from the publisher

This book was made possible thanks to the support of Michael J.J. Cowan

Text: Mark Goldie
Picture editor: Barry Phipps
Design: cantellday – www.cantellday.co.uk
Printer: Norwich Colour Print Ltd
Typeset in Gill Sans

Photographs: Stephen Bond (front cover, pp. 6, 23, 34, 42, 50, 53, 61, 62), Mark Gilbert (p. 14), Julia Hedgecoe (pp. 59 left, 67, 68, © 1996, 2008), Mark Miller (pp. 4, 49 left, 51, 54), Michel Pelletier (pp. 24, 25, 40), Barry Phipps (pp. 22, 26, 28, 30, 32, 33, 35, 37, 38, 39, 41, 44, 46, 47, 49 right, 57, 58, 64, 78), Peter Sutton (p. 48). Back cover montage: Stephen Bond (2nd, 9th), Chris Hicks (5th, 7th), Barry Phipps (1st, 3rd, 4th, 6th); the 5th and 7th images are of architect Quinlan Terry's drawings for metopes at Downing College Library. Images reproduced by courtesy of: Birmingham Mail (for whom Lew Williams was cartoonist, 1948-69) (p. 11), Cambridge Design Studio (p. 73), Hulton Archive/Getty Images (p. 8), Winston Churchill (pp. 9, 12-13), Gabriella Crick (pp. 12-13), Granada TV (p. 19), Nicholas Hawksworth (Wayfinding Consultants Ltd) (site plan, inside cover), Susan Lim (p. 21), Diana Parker (p. 20), Sheppard Robson (p. 27). Documents and images at pp. 8, 9, 10, 11, 12-13, 19, 27, 64 are held by the Churchill Archives Centre.

Back cover montage: shuttered concrete, which gives a surface texture of sawn wood; the star logo of the Maersk Company in the garden of the Møller Centre; Geoffrey Clarke's aluminium entrance gate; American donors to the Archives Centre (detail); radio telescope, developed by Nobel Laureate and Churchill Fellow Antony Hewish; the first Master, Sir John Cockcroft's Nobel Prize medal, awarded for splitting the atom; the double helix, unravelled by Nobel Laureate and Churchill Fellow Francis Crick; the squash courts wall in autumn; the principal staircase in the Møller Centre.

Visitors are welcome to visit those parts of the College that are not behind locked doors (but please do not enter residential staircases). Inclusion of an item in this Guide does not necessarily indicate public accessibility. Visitors to the Archives Centre and Møller Centre should call at their entrance desks. A key to the chapel may be borrowed from the Porters' Lodge.

FOREWORD

Churchill College is young by the standards of Cambridge University. Its architecture announces a self-consciously modern institution: there are no ivy-clad gothic walls here. Yet it already has a distinctive heritage and a patina of historical associations: there are, for instance, 20 buildings and rooms named after particular individuals.

This Guide is intended as an introduction to, and memento of, the College for visitors, students, parents, alumni, Fellows, staff, and prospective members, as well as an information resource for everyone interested in the College. It opens with an account of what is distinctive about Churchill. Part II describes the buildings and fabric, and the works of art on display, and identifies some of the people associated with them.

At the end are appendices giving further information, such as lists of distinguished Fellows and alumni. Every effort has been made to avoid errors, but corrections, additions, and suggestions for future editions will be gratefully received.

Mark Goldie

CONTENTS

Past and Present — 7
Essentials — 7
Origins — 7
Contexts of the creation — 9
College and University — 17
Governance — 17
Finance — 18
Staff — 18
Students — 19
Alumni — 20
Visitors — 21
Archives Centre — 21
Møller Centre — 22
Art collection — 23
Associated foundations — 25
Architecture — 26
Architecture: Møller Centre — 29
West Cambridge — 29

Guide to the Fabric — 31
The site — 31
Entrance — 31
Concourse — 32
Foyer — 33
Student Common Rooms — 33
Buttery — 33
Fellows' Gallery — 34
Senior Common Room — 35
Cockcroft Room — 35
Master's Lodge — 36
Fellows' Dining Room — 36
Main Staircase, Mezzanine, Dining Hall Foyer — 37
Tizard and Ashmore Rooms — 39

Offices — 40
Dining Hall — 40
Wolfson Hall — 41
Bracken and Bevin Libraries — 42
Archives Centre — 45
Great Court — 49
Residential Courts — 51
Fellows' and Master's Gardens — 52
Playing Fields — 52
Churchill Road — 52
Study Centre, Music Centre, Pavilion — 52
Møller Centre — 53
Sheppard Flats — 54
Chapel — 55
A Cambridge vista — 56
Wolfson Flats — 56
Broers, Bondi, and Hawthorne Houses — 56
Storey's Way — 59
Environs — 60

Appendices — 65
1. Chronology — 65
2. Masters — 66
3. Founder Trustees — 66
4. Honorary Fellows — 66
5. Distinguished Fellows — 67
6. Distinguished alumni — 72
7. Principal benefactors — 76
8. Buildings and architects — 76
9. Arms, motto, colours, grace, declaration — 77
10. Roskill memorial lecturers — 77
11. Archives Centre: principal collections — 78
12. Sir Winston Churchill's life — 80

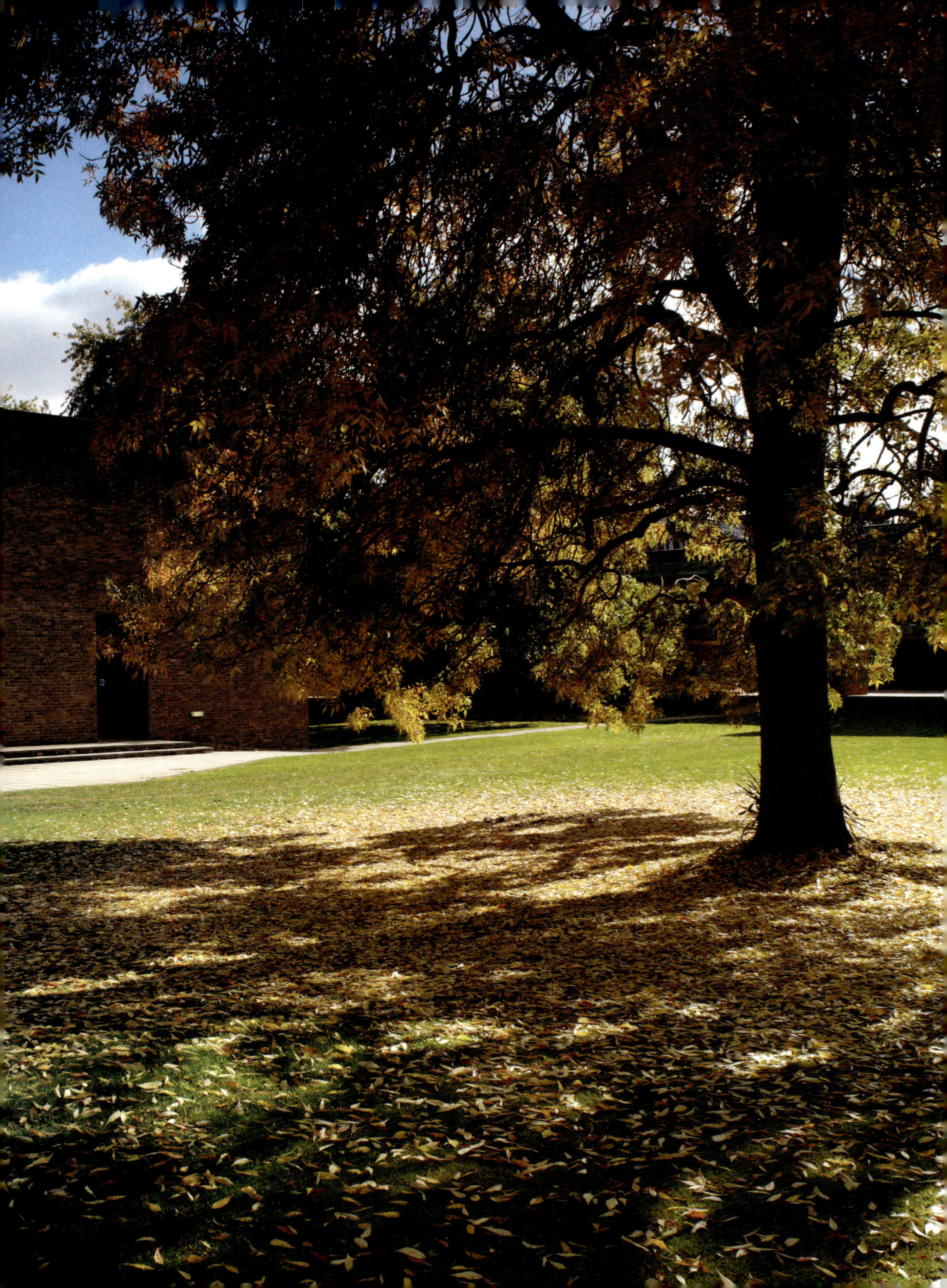

PAST AND PRESENT

Essentials

Churchill College is the national and Commonwealth memorial to Sir Winston Churchill, Britain's great wartime Prime Minister who led the struggle against Nazi tyranny. Founded by Royal Charter in 1960, the College is one of 31 constituent colleges of the University of Cambridge, which began 750 years earlier.

At its creation, the College was dedicated to three special purposes, to which it remains committed:

- an emphasis on science and technology, having a statutory requirement that 70 per cent of its students and academic staff are in the fields of natural or medical sciences, engineering, or mathematics;

- an emphasis on postgraduate education, having a statutory requirement that one-third of its students are studying for master's or doctoral degrees;

- an emphasis on visiting fellowships, having a scheme of Overseas Fellowships which has brought hundreds of distinguished scholars to Cambridge from around the world.

Within a dozen years of its establishment, the College acquired three further distinctive characteristics:

- it was the first men's college in Cambridge to make the decision to admit women;

- it pursued a meritocratic policy in undergraduate admissions, such that about three-quarters of its intake comes from schools in the state sector;

- it became the home of the Churchill Archives Centre, housing the Founder's papers, and later 600 further collections of key figures of the Churchill era and after.

Towards the close of the 20th century, the College added a final distinguishing feature:

- it established the Møller Centre for Continuing Education, to provide a venue for continuing professional development, especially for business and professional organisations.

Today the College is one of Cambridge's largest. It has around 150 Fellows, 250 postgraduates, and 450 undergraduates, together with 30 By-Fellows and 150 support staff. There is a world-wide community of over 7000 alumni. Sited in West Cambridge, in the University's expansion zone, it occupies a campus of 42 acres (17 hectares), the most extensive consolidated site of any Cambridge college.

Origins

Churchill College was the result of two independent projects in the 1950s for the promotion of advanced technological education, which unexpectedly came to fruition in Cambridge. In 1949 Winston Churchill visited Massachusetts Institute of Technology and expressed a

The Founder Trustees, meeting at Winston Churchill's London home in 1958

hope that a similar institution could be created in Britain. While on holiday in Sicily in 1955, after his retirement as Prime Minister, he had a conversation with Lord Cherwell (Frederick Lindemann), his wartime scientific advisor, and John Colville, his private secretary, in which Cherwell reminded him of his hope and urged that it was not too late to act; Colville promised to undertake the legwork. Meanwhile, several leading British industrialists had been meeting at the London headquarters of Shell Petroleum since 1950 to discuss the need for training advanced manpower in the sciences and engineering. They proposed an independent postgraduate institute with special syllabuses, to be based at Birmingham University or Cranfield Aeronautical College (now University), but these plans proved abortive. The American Carl Gilbert, chairman of Gillette Industries, together with the Cambridge Nobel Prizewinning chemist Alexander Todd, then recommended a Cambridge college of a special type, having a strong scientific and technological emphasis. To accommodate it within the University, the College would have undergraduates as well as postgraduates (postgraduate-only colleges did not then exist), and a proportion of members studying the humanities.

Accordingly, a new Cambridge college, the first to be named after a living person, was announced in 1958. A national appeal was launched to raise £3.5 million (equivalent to more than £50 million today) to build and endow Churchill College, chiefly directed at British industry, which produced the lion's share of donations. Major contributions were also received from the Ford, Gulbenkian, Rockefeller, and Wolfson Foundations, as well as the Transport and General Workers Union. Two thousand British companies and individuals contributed. Commonwealth and Continental European countries donated fabric and artwork. A body of Trustees was created, chaired by Sir Winston, comprising academics, industrialists, warriors, and statesmen. The University approved the scheme.

In 1959 a site in north-west Cambridge, one mile from the city centre, was chosen. Sir Winston paid his sole visit and planted two trees, but he never saw the built College. The Nobel physicist Sir John Cockcroft, who had split the atom in the Cavendish Laboratory in 1932, was appointed the College's first Master. After a limited competition, Richard Sheppard was selected as architect, and a College intended for 540 students and 60 Fellows was built in under a decade.

In 1960 the College received a Royal Charter and admitted its first students: two dozen postgraduates of a dozen nationalities. Undergraduates arrived the following year. The first buildings were completed in 1960, and the Dining Hall was inaugurated in 1964, marking the official opening. In 1966 Churchill achieved full status as a college of the University and the founder Trustees relinquished full governance to the Fellows.

Contexts of the creation

In a wider perspective, the College's origins are embedded in several contexts which reflect the British milieux of the mid-20th century. The founding reflected an anxiety, recurrent since the waning of the first Industrial Revolution, that British society did not nurture its technologists adequately, that achievement in pure science outstripped applied, and that economic and political leadership lay with members of the traditional professions, educated in the humanities, who disdained or ignored engineers and entrepreneurs.

When the College began, public debate became engulfed in the Two Cultures controversy, in which a founder Fellow, the novelist and scientific civil servant, C. P. Snow, crossed swords with the literary critic F. R. Leavis. Snow asked: Can inhabitants of the modern world call themselves civilised if they cannot state the second law of thermodynamics? It was a dramatic plea on behalf of scientific culture. Leavis thought Snow was a philistine and that Churchill College embodied a soulless technocratic utilitarianism.

The College is a living memorial, in honour of Winston Churchill, a quintessential British hero. In an important sense, the College's psychological birth lies in 1940, when Churchill became Prime Minister and Britain stood alone against Hitler. The College's third Master, Sir Hermann Bondi, an Austrian Jew who fled the Nazis, constantly spoke of civilisation having hung upon

```
                                              A.9
Since we have neither
    the massive population,

    nor the raw materials,

    nor yet adequate agricultural land
       to enable us to make our way
          in the world with ease,

we must depend for survival
    on our brains,

    on skilled minds
       that are at least proportionately
          equal to those in the
             United States and Soviet
                Russia.
=
This is far from being achieved,

    and even when it is,

    we shall only have reached
       a quantitative target.

In quality,

    we should endeavour to outstrip
       our friends and our rivals
          as we have done in the past.
```

Winston Churchill's sole visit to the site took place in 1959: his speech is typed out in his preferred 'psalm' style

C. P. Snow, founder Fellow, launched the Two Cultures controversy in 1959

a thread in 1940, and of the one man who held barbarism at bay. The national cult of Winston Churchill was at its peak when the College was conceived, and has waxed again in the 21st century: a BBC poll in 2002 voted Churchill 'the greatest Briton'. His secretary, Colville, wrote that 'the Battle of Britain of the future will be fought not on the beaches but in the laboratories'. Pride in wartime victory was allied to concern to find a new role. As Part II of this Guide reveals, the College's fabric carries many echoes of the conflicts of the mid-20th century.

The Second World War was a scientists' war, when a fraternity of Whitehall 'boffins' raced to achieve superiority in radar, air warfare, and the atom bomb. Like no other Prime Minister, Churchill understood the importance of science in war. The College's first, second, and third Masters, and many founder Fellows, belonged to that fraternity: not academics only, but scientists at war. Despite Snow's laments, scientists entered the corridors of power as never before. Snow's own work in civil service recruitment was vital, while his novels celebrated the 'New Men' of the atomic age. Pride in British science owed much to the pre-War heyday of nuclear physics, the golden age of Lord Rutherford's Cavendish Laboratory, which achieved 29 Nobel Prizes. The first Master, Cockcroft, was one of Rutherford's protégés. In the 1950s Cockcroft was one of Britain's best-known scientists, dubbed the 'atom chief'; and, partly to counter the sombre fact of Cold War nuclear weaponry, became a pundit for the 'peaceful atom', which promised limitless, cheap, clean, safe atomic energy. The College was officially opened in the same year as the leader of the Labour Party, Harold Wilson, won a general election with a slogan promising the 'white heat of the technological revolution'.

In the 1950s the Cold War was at its height, accompanied by an acute sense that the West was lagging behind the scientific achievements of the

RITAIN'S ATOM CHIEF.
3. Standing by the Cavendish cyclotron, the Sir John Cockcroft of to-day chats with Dr. A. E. Kempton. The machine gives atomic particles enormous speeds.

Sir John Cockcroft (right), the first Master, in the lab

LET'S FACE IT!   By Lewis Williams

"Let's look ahead a few years—you'll be asking me if I'm going on to college, and I'll be saying 'Yes—Churchill's'!"

The announcement of Winston Churchill's college attracts widespread media coverage, 1958

Soviet Union. Sputnik, the world's first space satellite, was launched in 1957, and caused near panic among Western policy-makers. In Britain and America money was pumped into university science and engineering. Churchill College was announced a year later, self-consciously seeking to counter the Soviet threat, Sir Winston urging all speed in training technologists for the West. Newspaper headlines linked Cambridge's new 'atom college' to the Communist threat.

At mid-century Britain lauded the ideal of 'meritocracy'. The word was coined by a founder Fellow of Churchill, the sociologist Michael (later Lord) Young, whose *Rise of the Meritocracy* (1958) envisaged a society in which jobs and rewards were geared to 'IQ + effort', a society where what counted was trained talent, rather than class, wealth, or inheritance. It was a progressive ideal, but not necessarily an egalitarian one, and contained echoes of H. G. Wells's futurist novels about a new technocratic

The Golden Helix,
19 Portugal Place,
Cambridge.

12th October, 1961.

Dear Sir Winston,

It was kind of you to write. I am sorry you do not understand why I resigned.

To make my position a little clearer I enclose a cheque for ten guineas to open the Churchill College Hetairae fund. My hope is that eventually it will be possible to build permanent accommodation within the College, to house a carefully chosen selection of young ladies in the charge of a suitable Madam who, once the institution has become traditional, will doubtless be provided, without offence, with dining rights at the high table.

Such a building will, I feel confident, be an amenity which many who live in the college will enjoy very much, and yet the instruction need not be compulsory and none need enter it unless they wish. Moreover it would be open (conscience permitting) not merely to members of the Church of England, but also to Catholics, Non-Conformists, Jews, Moslems, Hindus, Zen Buddhists and even to atheists and agnostics such as myself.

And yet I cannot help feeling that when you pass on my offer to the other Trustees – as I hope you will – they may not share my enthusiasms for such a truly educational project. They may feel, being men of the world, that to house such an Establishment, however great the need and however correctly conducted, within the actual College would not command universal respect. They may even feel my offer of ten guineas to be a joke in rather poor taste.

Continued.......

- 2 -

    But that is exactly my view of the proposal of the Trustees to build a chapel, after the middle of the 20th century, in a new College and in particular in one with a special emphasis on science. Naturally some members of the College will be Christian, at least for the next decade or so, but I do not see why the College should tacitly endorse their beliefs by providing them with special facilities. The churches in the town, it has been said, are half empty. Let them go there. It will be no further than they have to go to their lectures.

    Even a joke in poor taste can be enjoyed, but I regret that my enjoyment of it has entailed my resignation from the College which bears your illustrious name.

    Understandably I shall not be present on Saturday. I hope it all goes off well.

    Yours sincerely,

    Francis Crick

    F.H.C. Crick.

Sir Winston Churchill, K.G., M.P.,
Chartwell,
Westerham,
KENT.

LEFT and ABOVE: **Nobel Prize-winning biochemist Francis Crick's letter of resignation of his Fellowship in protest at the proposed building of a chapel. ('Hetairae' were ancient Greek courtesans)**

A student room – what else?

elite. In the post-War era, meritocracy was closely allied to faith in grammar schools as engines of social mobility, as against ancient 'public' (private) schools. Grammar schools, coupled with the arrival of universal state grants, enabled a new generation, who had demonstrated their 'IQ', to attend university, whose parents had not had the opportunity to do so. Michael Young was himself ambivalent about 'meritocracy' and his book was intended as a satire, but the term caught on and has often been used positively by politicians and social commentators. Young was the University's first lecturer in sociology, and Churchill College embraced several new disciplines disdained by older colleges: among its early Fellows were the University's first Professors of Operational Research and of Industrial Relations.

Mid-twentieth century Britain has been called a 'corporatist' state, in which government, industry, and trade unions combined in unison to achieve collective social aims, especially in industrial strategy and manpower planning. The Trade Unions became almost a department of government, as part of the consensual post-war settlement. In the later era of the Thatcherite free market, this regime would be regarded as economically sclerotic, and unions demonised as enemies of productivity. It is thus remarkable that the Transport and General Workers Union made a large donation to establish a Cambridge college, and that the President of the Amalgamated Engineering Union sat alongside captains of industry among its founder Trustees. The two parts of the College Library are named after a contrasting couple: an archetypal capitalist press baron, Brendan Bracken, and an archetypal socialist trade union boss, Ernest Bevin.

Looking further afield, we find that Winston Churchill's vaunting of Britain's 'Special Relationship' with the United States also made its impact on the College. American funds helped to create the College, especially the Archives Centre, which proudly displays the names of numerous American donors. The College's connection with the Winston Churchill Foundation of the United States is long-lasting, the Foundation sending an annual phalanx of talented Churchill Scholars. The College's Overseas Fellowship scheme has been dominated by Americans, visiting Cambridge for sabbatical research. In the 1950s Britain did not yet look toward a Continental European future. Only subsequently would the College, like the nation, begin to look eastwards, for instance to Denmark and France, with which the College has its closest European ties today.

These, then, were the contexts of the College's founding. A brief glance, next, at the 1960s and beyond. Three strands of national debate about higher education came home to roost in the College's early days. Traditionally, the ancient universities had taken a large percentage of their students from fee-paying private schools. The creation of universal state grants to cover fees and maintenance for university students made wider outreach possible. Churchill was one of the first colleges actively to pursue this opportunity, seeking talent first in state grammar schools and later in comprehensive schools. The issue of ensuring 'access' nevertheless endures, especially now that students are once more obliged to contribute financially toward their degree courses.

The second strand was the growing demand for greater opportunities for women in higher education. Until the late Victorian age, the ancient universities were for men only, and by 1960 there were still only three Cambridge women's colleges and none was co-educational. It seems odd today that Churchill was founded for men only, reflecting prevalent assumptions about women and science.

The College's decision to admit women unleashed a wave of reform: between 1972, when the first women students were admitted to Churchill, and 1986, one by one and often amid bitter wrangling, every formerly male college in Cambridge took the momentous decision to 'go mixed'.

Lastly, there was the question of the place of religion in a 'scientific age'. Here, the College was not immune from divisive controversy. Historically, the universities had been the seminaries of the church, and chapel attendance remained compulsory until the Second World War. Churchill's story is briefly told below, where the Chapel building is described, but the essence is that some founder Fellows were deeply hostile to the proposal to build a chapel, and Francis Crick, co-discoverer of the structure of DNA, resigned his Fellowship in protest. His letter to Winston Churchill explaining his resignation is one of the most bizarre ever sent by a great scientist to a great statesman:

Alison Finch, Fellow in French literature, Vice-Master, pictured in the 1970s shortly after election as one of the first women Fellows

CHURCHILL COLLEGE CAMBRIDGE

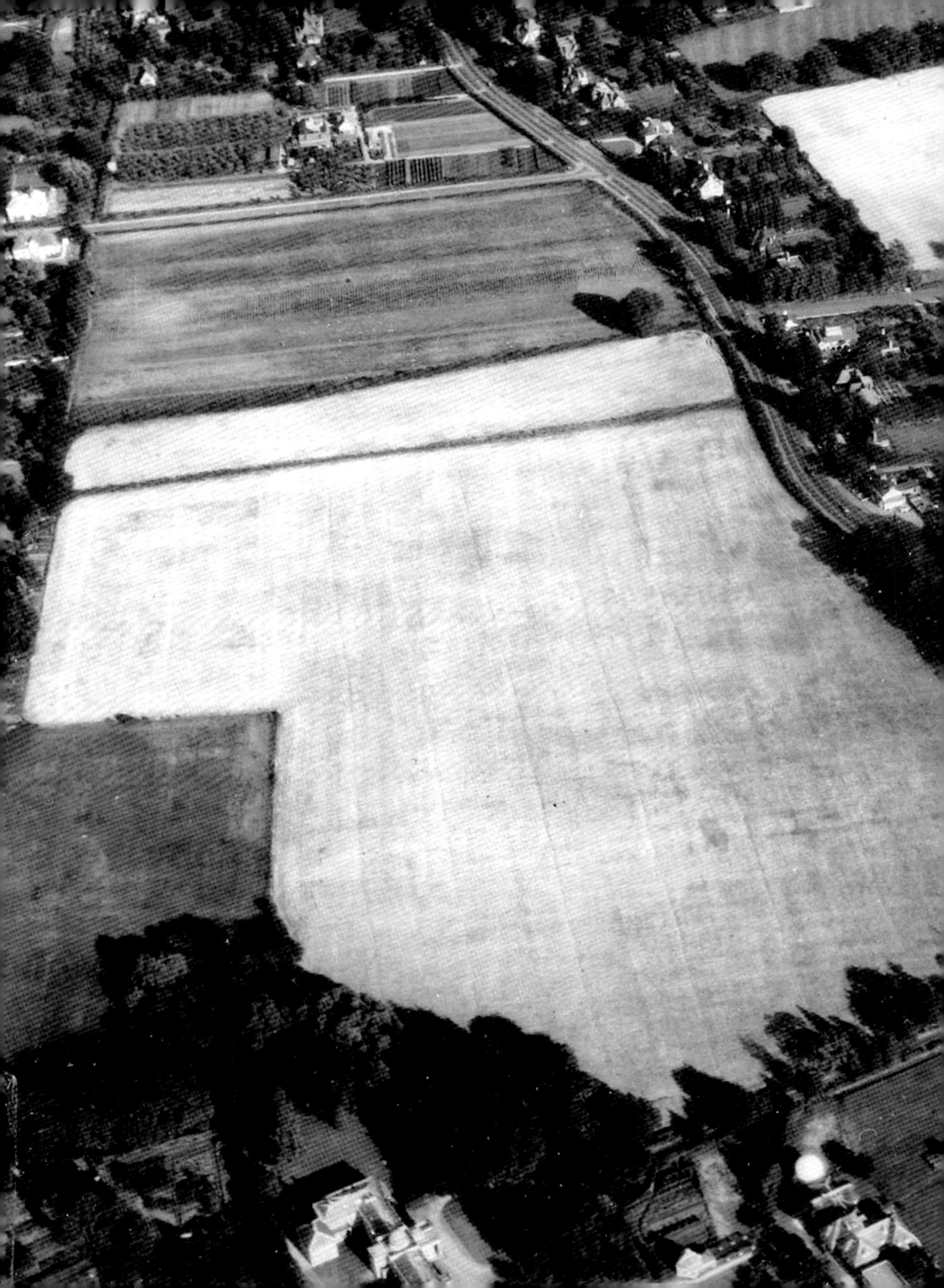

Crick opined that a College brothel would be more worthwhile than a chapel. The outcome of the controversy was that a chapel was built in the grounds but is not an official part of the College. A preposition saved the day: it was agreed there would be a chapel *at* Churchill but not *of* Churchill.

Within a decade of its founding, the College had acquired its distinctive character. If the Founder's vast archive had not yet arrived, the creation of the Churchill Archives Centre was already mooted. And if the Møller Centre for Continuing Education would follow much later, it also had its roots in another aspiration of the founder Trustees: that there should be scope for continuing professional development and educational programmes in management.

College and University

Several universities have constituent colleges but those at Cambridge and Oxford are unique in the extent of their autonomy: they are much more than halls of residence. Self-governing corporations, empowered by Royal Charter, they have their own endowments and control admission of their members, both junior (students) and senior (Fellows). Colleges vary in size, wealth, and academic emphasis, but all admit students in practically every discipline, so that each college is a miniature *universitas*.

Accordingly, Cambridge University is a complex federation comprising academic departments and residential colleges. The University awards degrees, structures academic courses, organises research, and provides part of undergraduate teaching – lectures and laboratory classes. The colleges provide residential, social, sporting, and welfare facilities, and organise another key part of teaching – tutorials, known as supervisions. Colleges are less academically important for postgraduates, but remain vital in providing accommodation and community, especially in a university with a preponderance of overseas postgraduates. Most academic staff of the University 'wear two hats', holding posts as professors, readers, lecturers, or postdoctoral researchers in departments, and also Fellowships in colleges. Colleges have a special role in providing post-doctoral Fellowships, key stepping-stones to academic careers, and also College Lectureships, which support undergraduate teaching. A college is a place to exchange ideas across disciplines, to energise and support students, and to socialise. Colleges make Cambridge far more encompassing than a nine-to-five campus, and humanise a university that has 20,000 members.

Governance

Like other colleges, Churchill College is a participatory republic, having a Master as presidential head, academic Fellows who sit on governing committees, together with representation of other 'estates': students of the 'junior' and 'middle' common rooms, and support staff. Churchill shares with Trinity College the fact that its Master is appointed by the Crown, through the Prime Minister, although Downing Street these days inclines to follow the Fellows' wishes. Churchill is unique in having non-academic staff statutorily represented on its College Council. The Governing Body comprises all Fellows other than Overseas and Emeriti and meets about six times a year. The Council has 19 members, seven *ex officio* and others elected, and is the principal executive body, meeting about 15 times a year; under new charity law, its members are the College's trustees. Four student representatives sit on Governing Body and Council, and two non-academic staff members on Council. The Council appoints teaching Fellows, while a committee called the Fellowship Electors appoints Fellows in other categories. There are seven types of Fellow: Teaching, Research, Professorial, Emeritus, Extraordinary, Overseas, and Supernumerary. In addition there are Honorary Fellows.

LEFT: The College site in 1960 before building, looking east, the University Observatory in the foreground

The Master chairs the principal committees, is the College's voice and representative on public occasions, and is involved in outreach among alumni and the wider world. Generally, the Mastership is part-time and, typically, the holder also holds a professorship in a University department. Besides the Master, the College's principal officers are the Senior Tutor, who oversees undergraduate education and welfare; the Tutor for Advanced Students, who similarly serves postgraduates; the Vice-Master, who deals with Fellowship matters; and the Bursar, who has charge of operational matters, finance, and facilities. There are 12 personal tutors, who counsel students, and three Admissions Tutors, who manage applications for undergraduate places. There are 28 Directors of Studies, one (or more) for each degree course ('Tripos'), who ensure that undergraduates are provided with tutorial teaching and perform to their best. These do not exhaust the tasks assigned to Fellows. There is a President of the Senior Common Room and a Steward (for social matters), a Dean (for discipline), Praelector (for presentation of students for degrees), Librarian, Director of Music-Making, and Development Director (for alumni relations and fundraising). Churchill has no chaplain; instead there is a professional counsellor (the Chapel Trust, however, appoints its own chaplain). The College has a Visitor, an honorific role: Prince Philip, the Duke of Edinburgh. Committees attend to every aspect of College life: the Finance, Education, Estates, Welfare, and Hanging (art) committees, to name a few. While most academic administration remains the part-time avocation of Fellows whose prime responsibilities are to teaching and research, there is a growing tendency, as in other colleges, for leading roles, such as Senior Tutor and Bursar, to become full-time.

The College's governance is determined by its Charter, Statutes, Ordinances, and Regulations. The Charter and Statutes may be amended by permission of the Crown's Privy Council. From a constitutional point of view, Cambridge colleges are a paradoxical and very British hybrid: they are autonomous republics but ones created by royal prerogative. Churchill College has amended its Charter just once, to delete the clause restricting membership to men.

Finance

Churchill College's assets in 2008 were estimated to be worth £115 million, comprising £75 million in tangible assets (mainly the site and its buildings) and £40 million in its investment portfolio, chiefly in equities and commercial property. (Owing to a generous donation of shares, there has always been a significant holding in Associated British Foods, which owns Primark and British Sugar, and such brands as Ovaltine, Ryvita, and Twinings). The College ranks just below half way in the wealth table of Cambridge colleges. The College's income in 2007-8 was £9.6 million. There are five main sources of income: rental, meals, and other charges to members (32%); academic fees, mainly from public authorities and national research councils (22%); investment income (19%); donations (16%); and income and gift aid from the Møller Centre and the College's conference business (11%). The chief areas of expenditure are: staff salaries, catering, utilities and rates, maintenance of the fabric, teaching and tutorial payments, studentships, scholarships, bursaries, alumni relations, and the Archives Centre. The Møller Centre is a College-owned subsidiary company. Most of the academic staff (university lecturers, readers, and professors) receive their prime salaries from the University, but the College also employs College lecturers, postdoctoral research fellows, and academic administrators.

Staff

In Cambridge nomenclature, 'staff' means non-academic staff, as in the phrase 'Fellows and staff'. The College depends on its support staff, of whom there are around 150, organised into departments: office, catering, computing, conference, library, finance, maintenance, grounds and gardens, porters' lodge, and housekeeping, together with the Archives Centre. In addition, the Møller Centre has a separate staff of 60. The staff includes (to name just some) a Registrar, Conference Manager, Computer Systems Manager, Head Porter, Housekeeper, Dining Hall Manager, Nurse, Finance Manager, Catering Manager, Maintenance Manager, Librarian, Development Director, Alumni

The College's winning University Challenge team, 1970: John Armytage, Gareth Aicken, Meredith Lloyd-Evans, Malcolm Keay.

Relations Manager, Student Recruitment Officer, and Boatman. In keeping with Cambridge tradition, there are 'bedmakers' who look after residential rooms. The half-century of the College's history has seen a transition from a world in which colleges were still modelled on ancient country houses, with posts like Butler, to one in which they are modelled on businesses: by the mid 2000s the College had a Director of Hospitality Services. This change has much to do with the growing importance of conference, professional training, and hotel-style revenue streams, together with an increasing perception by students and parents of themselves as 'consumers' of higher education, as well as the changing character of the academic profession.

Students

School and college students who apply to become undergraduates mention five main reasons for choosing Churchill: that it is modern; provides on-site accommodation to every student throughout their course; takes a high number of students from the state sector; specialises in science and engineering; and has all its facilities and playing fields on a single site. Applicants are not, however, obliged to select a college and can instead make an 'open' application to the University, to be allotted for consideration by a college via a computer algorithm. Furthermore, a proportion of the College's students are selected from the University's inter-collegiate 'Pool' of those candidates who are unsuccessful in applications to more heavily subscribed colleges. Admission is based on interview and academic record, and is normally conditional on achieving top grades in public exams. Nearly all undergraduates have achieved three (or more) grade A's at A-level, or its equivalent in other exams, such as the International Baccalaureate. Like other colleges, Churchill receives about four to five applications per place, though ratios vary considerably by subject, and application patterns are volatile from year to year. Deferred entry (following a 'gap year') is welcomed. The College admits students in every University course ('Tripos') except Land Economy and Theology. Since the 1970s College members have funded a Southern African Bursary to provide places for black African students.

Colleges are preoccupied with their ratings in annual (unofficial) University league table showing academic performance. Churchill rode highest in the 1970s and 1980s, when it enjoyed the cachet, then still unusual, of admitting women and attracting the best talent from state schools. Other colleges have since caught up, but Churchill remains in the top quarter or third of colleges.

Among the College's postgraduates, around 60 per cent are studying for PhDs and 40 for Master's degrees. Churchill is unusual in having extensive residential accommodation on site for students with partners and families (itself a daring innovation in the

1960s). The University is approximately stable in undergraduate numbers but expanding in the postgraduate sector, especially in one-year Master's courses. Today, one third of the University's students are postgraduates, reflecting the proportion that Churchill has had since its inception, but Churchill's ratio remains unusual, since specialist postgraduate colleges account for a significant proportion of the University's overall numbers. Around two-thirds of the College's postgraduates are non-British citizens, representing a very different profile from the undergraduate body.

Students self-organise much of their social life, and their interests are represented by elected officers and committees, led by the Presidents of the Junior and Middle Common Rooms. Their officers include those for Access, Entertainments, Women's Welfare, Men's Welfare, 'LGBT' Welfare, Environment, and Editor of the student magazine, *Winston*. Of the numerous clubs and societies, Churchill is particularly known in the wider University for its student club night (the 'Pav') and as the locale of the University radio station; formerly, it was known for its Film Club. The College has exceptional music facilities. 'Sizars', chosen annually, organise activities in music, drama, and the visual arts. In rowing, the highest place achieved by the men's first boat in the 'May Bumps' was 6th (in 2006); the women's first boat was Head of the River six times between 1978 and 1990. The football team headed the university league for two years, 2005-7. Three examples of recent student achievements are: a fencer at the Beijing Olympics; the winner of the BBC national student radio award for best female presenter; and worldwide news coverage of the Spaceflight Society's launch of teddy bears into space from the College grounds.

Alumni

Every walk of life is represented among the College's alumni. As graduates of a predominantly scientific college, there is a natural emphasis on the worlds of technology, engineering, life sciences, and business; yet there is also strong representation in the arts, media, and public service. As a young college, it was not until the 1990s that its alumni began to scale the heights in public life. The College acquired its first chief executives of major companies, high court judge, ambassador, bishop, leading professional authors, and a couple of Members of Parliament. In 2007, for the first time, the College elected an alumnus to an Honorary Fellowship; in 2008 a former postgraduate won the Nobel Prize for Chemistry; by 2009 one hundred alumni were entered in *Who's Who*. All alumni are regularly invited to return for reunions, and enjoy lifetime rights to dine and stay in College. Alumni automatically belong to the Churchill Association and receive annual newsletters and the *Churchill Review*. Around the turn of the 21st century, Churchill, like other colleges, began to place more emphasis on alumni relations, as well as on fundraising, through its Development Office. The financial future lies less with the state and more with corporate and alumni donations, in the new national regime of student debt and university 'top-up' fees, and given the College's commitment to provide accommodation for every student and a wide range of bursaries.

Diana Parker, alumna, the first woman chairman of a leading London law firm

Susan Lim, alumna, the first surgeon successfully to perform a liver transplant in Asia

Visitors

The College's substantial visiting fellowships programme provides invaluable opportunities for international collaborative research. Overseas Fellows, in residence for periods of one term to one year, are senior academics on sabbatical leave from their own universities. Additionally, visiting By-Fellows come into residence for shorter periods, including academics from Britain and abroad, researchers in the Archives Centre, schoolteachers, and artists-in-residence, as well as professional and business people. Members of the public are welcomed to exhibitions and special lectures. The Wolfson Hall is used by, for example, the Society for the Application of Research, the National Association of Decorative and Fine Arts Societies, and the annual lecture of the Cambridge Branch of the British Red Cross. The Møller Centre provides a year-round management, conference, and training centre for a large number of corporate training programmes, and seminars – academic, professional, commercial, medical, and cultural. Besides the Centre, the main body of the College sees many visitors through its conference service.

Archives Centre

The Churchill Archives Centre is a unique institution in Cambridge and the nearest British equivalent of the American presidential libraries. It is a major research institute for the study of 20th-century British history and attracts historians from around the world. It is one of the few purpose-built archive centres in Britain. The Centre is financially independent, and funded by the Churchill College Archives Trust, the Sir Winston Churchill and Margaret Thatcher Archive Trusts, grants from charitable and research foundations, and donations from philanthropic individuals. Opened in 1973, the Centre employs a staff of ten, including the Director, archivists, and conservators.

At the Centre's heart are its strongrooms, housing around 40,000 boxes of archives. These rooms are air-conditioned and humidity-controlled, and equipped with mobile and fire-resistant shelving, and sophisticated security and fire prevention systems. In the Conservation Workshop preventative and remedial work is carried out on fragile papers. There is an exhibition hall (the Jock Colville Hall), reading rooms for 10 researchers, and a suite of offices where archivists catalogue papers and respond to enquiries. An outreach programme encompasses exhibitions, open days, and online documentary educational resources. Exhibitions are mounted elsewhere and in partnership, such as with the National Library of Scotland and the Library of Congress in Washington DC. President George W. Bush opened the 'Churchill and the Great Republic' exhibition at the latter in 2004.

There are 600 collections, almost all pertaining to 20th-century political, scientific, and military figures. Although personal archives, they often contain official material, and the Centre has 'designated status' from the Museums, Libraries, and Archives Council as a collection of 'national and international importance'.

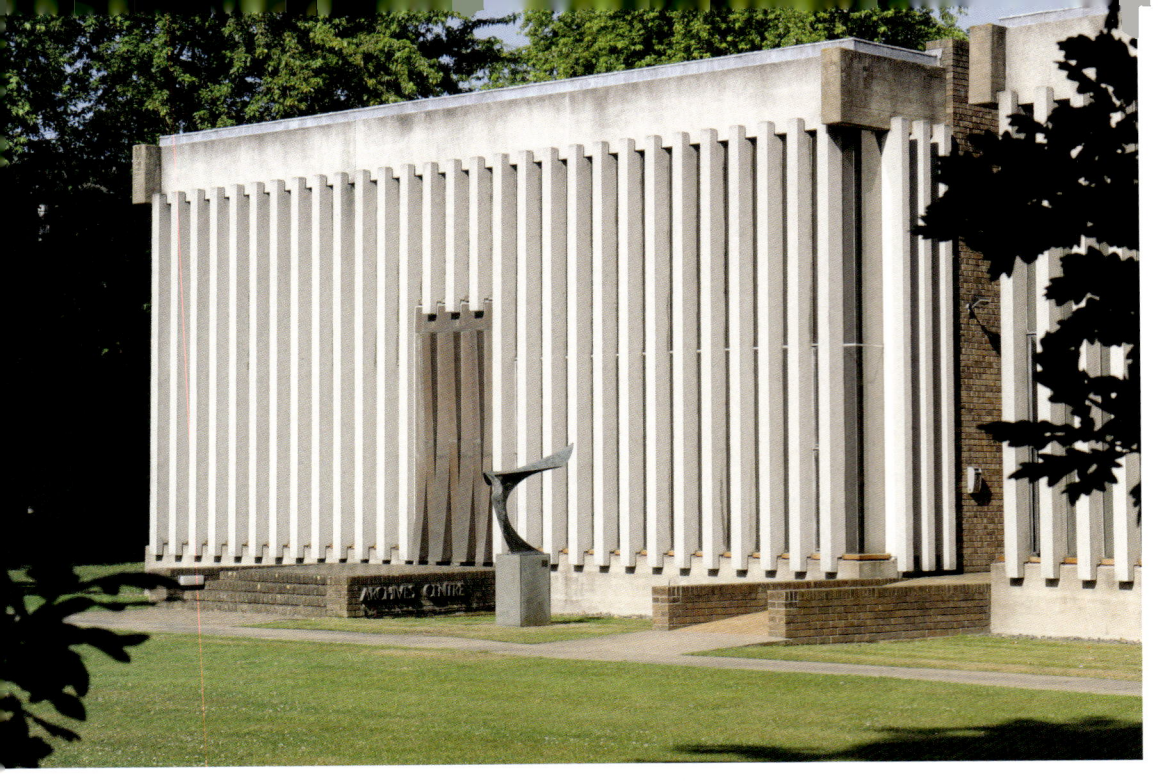

The Archives Centre, created to house Sir Winston Churchill's papers

The Centre's core collection is Winston Churchill's papers: over 2,500 boxes of letters and documents ranging from early childhood letters, through wartime speeches, to his last writings when in retirement. Scholarly access to these papers became possible in 1992, with the completion of Sir Martin Gilbert's official biography. A National Heritage Lottery grant in 1995 secured the collection for the nation and supported an on-line catalogue. The papers of Conservative Prime Minister Margaret Thatcher were acquired in 1997 and of Labour Leader Neil Kinnock in 1992.

Other collections include those of the Nobel Prize-winning scientists Sir James Chadwick, Sir John Cockcroft, and Sir Martin Ryle; those of two Nobel contenders, the physicist Lise Meitner and biochemist Rosalind Franklin; as well as the inventor of the jet engine Sir Frank Whittle. The Centre's catalogues can be accessed via the College's website. The British Diplomatic Oral History programme is supported by the Centre.

Among the Centre's documentary highlights are a signed photograph of Adolf Hitler, and his personal notepaper, a seating plan from the Potsdam conference with Joseph Stalin's signature, the original texts of Winston Churchill's 'Finest Hour' and 'Iron Curtain' speeches, and an account of the last official flogging in the British Navy.

Although the Centre is not a museum, it has a small number of notable artefacts, such as Sir John Cockcroft's Nobel Prize medal, a bronze cast of Winston Churchill's hand, ministerial despatch boxes, one of Prime Minister Thatcher's famous handbags, Sir Frank Whittle's sliderule, and graphite from one of the earliest nuclear reactors, at Oak Ridge, Tennessee, which provided enriched uranium for the first atomic bomb.

Møller Centre

When the College was founded, it was envisaged that it would offer not only standard university courses, but also 'in-service' training for employees in industry and vacation courses in business management for undergraduates, at a time when management scarcely existed as an academic discipline. The accent on adult education found expression in Michael Young's experiments in providing courses at Churchill for members of the public who had missed out on a university education, which led to the creation of the Open University in 1969. In general, however, the founding aspiration for close links with industry was not initially achieved.

With the opening of the Møller Centre in 1992 the original ambition began to be realised in new form. The Centre is independent from the university curriculum and provides a venue for external commercial and professional clients. Originally called 'The Møller Centre for Continuing Education', it now styles itself the 'Møller Centre: Management Training and Conference Centre'. The building was made possible by a gift of £10 million from the Danish merchant shipping and logistics entrepreneur, Maersk McKinney Møller, through the A. P. Møller and Chastine McKinney Møller Foundation, to mark his admiration for Winston Churchill's wartime achievement. The company pioneered the containerisation revolution and 'Maersk' containers ply the world's seaways, railways, and motorways. The Maersk star logo is reproduced in the box-hedged garden by the Centre's entrance.

The Centre was launched with the conviction that education must increasingly be lifelong, every profession needing periodically to update and retool. The Centre works alongside and plays host to programmes from the University's Institute of Continuing Education, the Cambridge Programme for Sustainability Leadership, the Judge Business School, and the Institute of Manufacturing, in providing for industrial, commercial, and professional career development. It chiefly hosts programmes constructed by client organisations, but also develops its own in-house programmes for overseas clients, particularly from China. The Centre's focus is on executive education and clients come from a range of sectors, such as FT500 companies, small and medium enterprises, the public sector, and academic institutions.

The Centre operates as a limited company wholly owned by the College, and transfers its profits to the College. The Centre also owns and operates the adjacent Study Centre. The architecture and building is described below and in Part II.

Art Collection

The College's art collection numbers over 400 items, of which about 80 belong to the Maisonneuve Bequest. The artworks on continuous display are mentioned in Part II below and this note provides a summary of the collection as a whole. Older paintings include: two by Winston Churchill: 'The Atlantic, near Biarritz' (1931) and 'Orchids' (1948); a landscape by Maximilien Luce, 'The Avenue' (1903); and a portrait of Edmund Burke attributed to George Romney

The Møller Centre, created to provide continuing professional development

'The Avenue' by Maximilien Luce

(c.1785). There are drawings and prints by André Derain, Duncan Grant, Barbara Hepworth, Paul Hogarth, Federico Garcia Lorca, Eduardo Paolozzi, Bridget Riley, and Henri Toulouse-Lautrec. It is perhaps less the paintings than other works which are the most artistically significant, especially sculptures by Émile Bourdelle, Barbara Hepworth, Bernard Meadows, Dhruva Mistry, and Denis Mitchell, as well as Geoffrey Clarke metalwork, John Piper glass, and a Lurçat tapestry. The benefaction by Pierre Maisonneuve is chiefly of French post-Impressionist paintings. In keeping with its commitment to Modernism, the College displays only abstract sculptures in exterior spaces; representational works are reserved for the interiors. In addition to works owned or on permanent loan, the College benefits from major sculptures, paintings, and prints on shorter loans from generous owners.

Among some 20 depictions of Winston Churchill, there are four busts in bronze, by Franta Belsky, Jacob Epstein, Oscar Nemon, and W. Reid Dick; and two portraits, by John Gilroy and John Leigh-Pemberton. In addition, the College has prints by Feliks Topolski, cartoons by Vicky, and an engraving from a photograph by Yousuf Karsh. A portrait of Churchill by John Wilson Jowsey is on permanent loan to the English Speaking Union and hangs at Dartmouth House, London. For depictions of Churchill, see Ronald Smith, *Churchill: Images of Greatness* (1989).

Portraits of people associated with the College include: Athanassiades Bodossakis (A. Materas, 1973), Sir Hermann Bondi (June Mendoza, 1989), Sir John Boyd (Tom Phillips, 2008), Brendan Bracken (Sir Edwin Lutyens), Lord (Alec) Broers (Jason Sullivan, 1996), Sir Edward Bullard (Ursula Bullard, 1978), Sir John Cockcroft (Robert Tollast, 1962), Lady (Elizabeth) Cockcroft (Robert Tollast, 1962), Noel Duckworth (Pamela Townshend, 1973), Sir William Hawthorne (Rodrigo Moynihan, 1984), Richard Hey (Nikolai Nikogosian, 1982), Kenneth McQuillen (Dora Boneva, 1970), Stephen Roskill (Michael Noakes, 1978), Sir Charles Snow (Michael Ayrton,

1963); Sir Barnes Wallis (A. E. Cooper, 1953), Sir Isaac Wolfson (Robert Tollast, 1965). See 'Tizard Room' below, for further Tollast drawings.

Brendan Bracken bequeathed furniture, which includes an 18th-century corner sideboard, mostly kept in the Master's Lodge, Cockcroft Room, and Senior Common Room. The College owns a 5th-century BCE Corinthian drinking vessel.

The College's silver collection, some of which is on display at feasts, is extensive: some 130 items or sets. The Hanoverian items (tea and coffee sets, salvers, etc.), and the oldest items (two Charles II patch boxes) were gifts from Bracken, but gone are the days when his cigar and snuff boxes were circulated (nor is his port railway in use). Two items are especially iconic. The 'atomic rose bowl' is a gift of Sir John Cockcroft: the juxtaposition of the atom and rose water symbolises 1950s hopes for the peaceful application of atomic power (the atom is boron, which is used in cooling rods in nuclear reactors). The Williamsburg Liberty Bell was presented to Winston Churchill in 1955 in recognition of his contribution to the struggle for freedom. The collection includes sets of Churchill centenary medals. Hugh Clarke bequeathed an extensive table service. The Governments of Denmark and Norway (1963-4) presented fruit bowls (and the former a dinner service for use at High Table). Strikingly stylish are items designed by Robert Welch, including a coffee urn, with stand and burner, jug and sugar bowl (1960), gift of Cockcroft, exhibited in 'The Pleasures of Peace: Mid-Century Craft and Art in Britain', Sainsbury Centre, Norwich, 1999. A severely modernist candelabrum, 74 cm tall (Desmond Clem-Murphy, 1967), presented by Williamson Cliff, Stamford, the College's brickmakers, provides a centrepiece at High Table.

Associated foundations

The Winston Churchill Foundation of the United States, founded in 1959, has, throughout the College's life, funded a cohort of Winston Churchill Scholars to study at Churchill for postgraduate degrees in the sciences (400 to date), as well as supporting the Archives Centre. A different body, the Winston Churchill Memorial Trust

'Orchids' by Winston Churchill

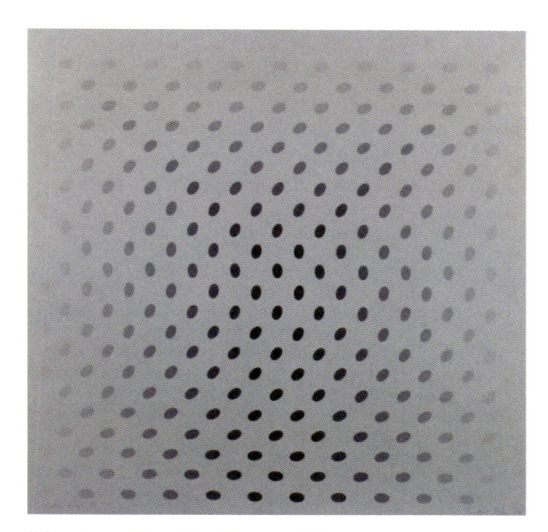

'Nineteen Greys' by Bridget Riley

of the United Kingdom, provides members of the British public with opportunities for educational travel, and has representatives from the College on its board; since 2006 it has provided 30 bursaries annually to College students. A number of organisations and individuals fund named Fellowships and studentships, just one example of which is the Winton Foundation's Professorship in the Public Understanding of Risk.

Churchill College's 'sister college' in Oxford, with whom it enjoys reciprocal arrangements, is Trinity College (though the Oxford college that is most akin

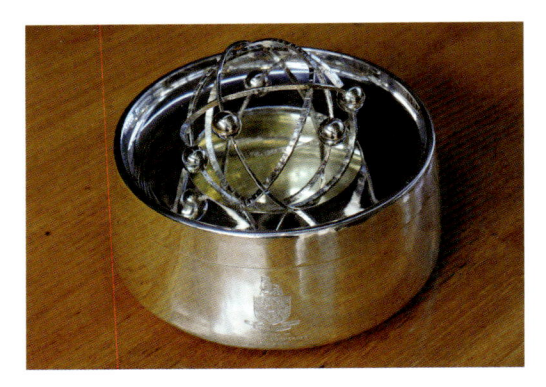

The atomic rose bowl

to Churchill, in origins and architecture, is St Catherine's. There are also reciprocal faculty relations with the Technion Institute in Haifa. The French Cultural Delegation nominates visiting Fellows, and the Danish Carslberg Foundation formerly did so. There are student exchanges with the Massachusetts Institute of Technology and the French École Centrale.

The Archives Centre, as the principal locale for the study of Winston Churchill, has close relations with other Churchillian sites, such as the Cabinet War Rooms and Churchill Museum in Whitehall, and Chartwell (Winston's family home) in Kent. Other Churchillian sites are his birthplace and place of burial, Blenheim Palace and Bladon churchyard, near Oxford; and the secret wartime codebreaking establishment at Bletchley Park in Milton Keynes. The International Churchill Society keeps Winston's memory alive, and the College maintains a close association with Winston's descendants, particularly with the Founder's daughter Lady Soames.

Architecture

Churchill College was the first Cambridge college to take the plunge into architectural modernism. British universities were slow to adopt modernism, preferring neo-classical and neo-gothic styles. In 1959 the competition to select an architect to design the College was one of the most important of the post-war era, providing an entry point to university work for rising practices, many of whom subsequently built the new universities of the 1960s. Twenty firms were invited to submit designs, all modernists, even though Winston Churchill is known to have preferred something classical. The winner was Richard Sheppard (1910-82), of Sheppard, Robson and Partners, who had hitherto specialised in designing schools for local authorities; his principal assistant for Churchill was William Mullins (1927-). The three other finalists were Howell, Killick and Partridge; James Stirling and James Gowan; and Chamberlin, Powell, and Bon. Sir Nikolaus Pevsner, author of the *Buildings of England* series, enthused that Churchill College was 'an outstanding conception', 'the best of the new'. Since some had proposed skyscrapers or massive single-courtyard megastructures, Sheppard's was by no means the most radical design, and the architectural historian Elain Harwood judges the College, as built, to be 'conservatively majestic'. It combines a modernist vocabulary and use of materials with an almost wilfully romantic and unregimented ground plan, while remaining faithful to the traditional Oxbridge principle of the courtyard.

Modernists aspired to functional simplicity and elementary geometry, and experimented with new materials, notably concrete. They jettisoned historical references and eschewed ornament. Sheppard's aesthetic lies in the massing of his buildings and texture of his materials. There is a heroic purity in the massive, uninterrupted brick walls of the Dining Hall and squash courts, and in the serried ranks of tall, slim, concrete mullions in the Library and Dining Hall windows. The residential courts are modest and domestic in scale, but there is monumentality in the great Dining Hall, Cambridge's largest, and in the twin brick pylons at the entrance. The device most characteristic of its era is shuttered concrete, achieved by pressing wooden planks against wet concrete so that the pattern of natural wood remains. The use of exposed concrete was called 'brutalism', but at Churchill it is married to extensive use of a warm, brown, vernacular Stamfordstone brick. The strongest influence on Sheppard was the guru of modernism, Le Corbusier. The horizontal banding of concrete and brick, and the Hall's vaulted concrete arches, echo Corbusier's iconic Maisons Jaoul, Paris (1953-5).

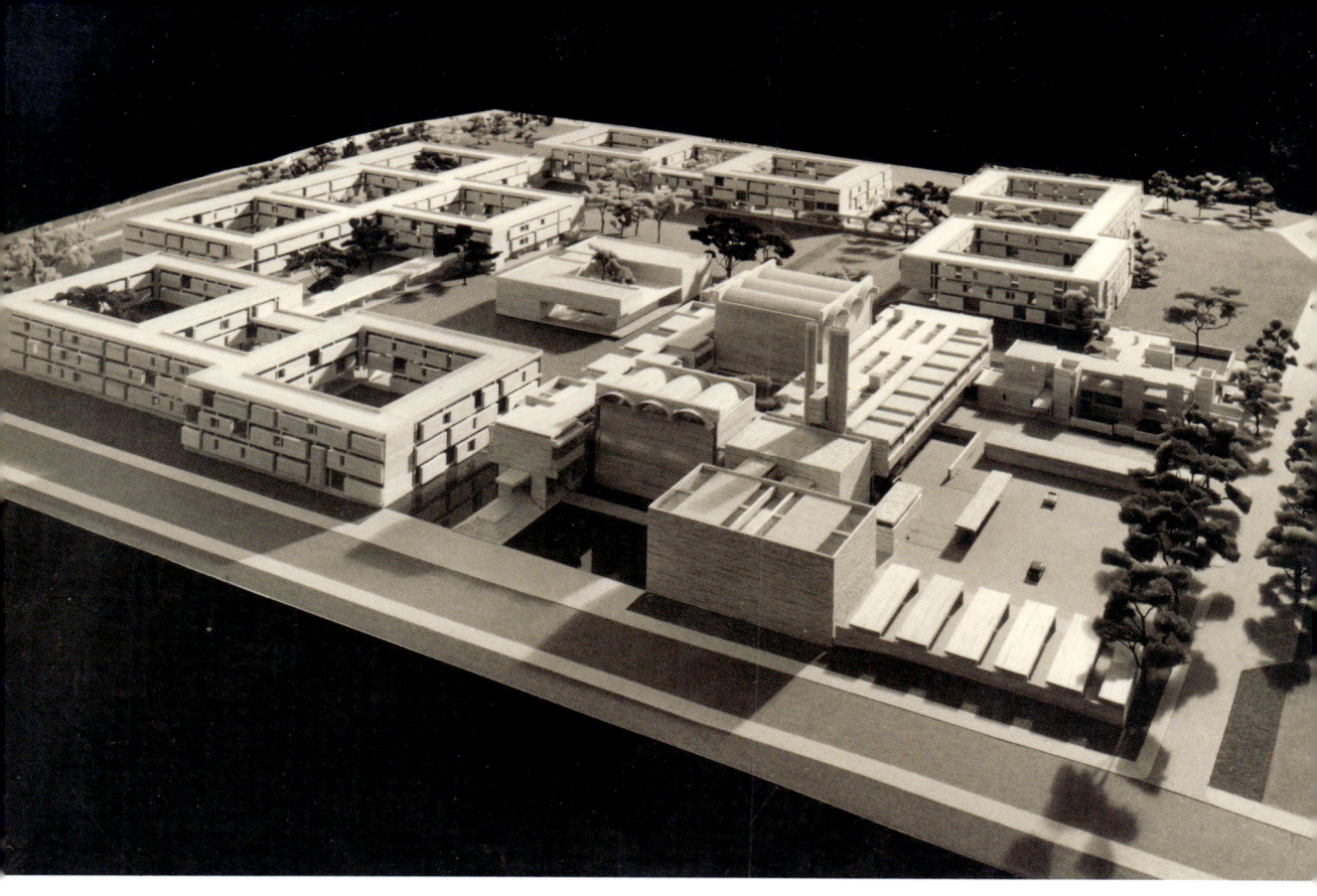

Richard Sheppard's model scheme for the College, showing courtyards and chapel that were never built

Although the design is modern, the plan of the residential areas reflects a fidelity to the ancient collegiate idea: intimate, interlocking courtyards, with self-contained staircases (rather than corridors). There is a surprising individuality to each room, and plenty of open vistas across the lawns. The masterstroke is the provision to nearly every room of a cantilevered oriel window, housing a terrazzo marble window seat, a feature beloved by residents. Many rooms have narrow vertical slit windows, a 1960s affectation. There are 10 interlinked courtyards, grouped in threes, except for the last one built, which is solitary. Each trio consists of two courts (23 sq. m., 75 ft) with sunken lawns (or, rather, raised walkways) and a smaller (17 sq. m., 55 ft) paved middle court. The staircases (usually six per larger courtyard) are externally visible and toplit; typically with 12 rooms each, and stairs with precast concrete treads. As in older colleges, student bedsitting rooms are interspersed with Fellow's offices and residential flats ('sets'). A further proposed trio of courts, which would have enclosed the central Great Court and blocked the westward view across the playing fields, was never built; the College would now never contemplate closing off the western vista. Instead a single, tenth, court was created, this time without a sunken lawn.

Circulation around the courts takes the form of a modern interpretation of the medieval cloister, with rooms cantilevered overhead. The avoidance of lift access confined the height to three storeys (with just two storeys in some of the linking ranges). The necklace of courtyards surrounds the Great Court, though the impression of there being a 'Great Court' is interrupted by communal buildings placed in its centre.

Richard Sheppard and William Mullins designed the main body of the College, starting with the Sheppard Flats at the far west end (1960-1) and ending with the

The College from the playing fields, looking east towards central Cambridge, pinnacles of King's College Chapel just visible

Archives Centre (1971-3). The contractor was Rattee and Kett, a subsidiary of Mowlem, except for the Sheppard Flats, built by Bernard Sunley and Sons. Several later architects have built on the site, listed in Appendix 8. In 1993 Churchill College was among the first group of half-dozen post-war buildings in the University to be accorded 'listed' status by government as being of 'special architectural or historic interest'.

Most of the original furniture, curtains, and carpets in the public rooms were designed by Robin Day (1915-) and Lucienne Day (1917-). Described in an exhibition at the Barbican Art Gallery in 2001 as 'Britain's most revered and accomplished designers of the post-war period', Robin Day's 1963 polyprop stacking chair is the world's most successful chair ever. The couple studied at the Royal College of Art and married in 1942. The crisp and angular geometry of Robin Day's furniture, some still in use, complements the architecture. Lucienne Day's curtains (a sample in the Whitworth Art Gallery, Manchester) and carpets do not survive. See Lesley Jackson, *Robin and Lucienne Day: Pioneers of Contemporary Design* (2001). The original landscape designer was Sheila Haywood, ARIBA, AILA, of London. The College's architecture is further explored in Mark Goldie, *Corbusier Comes to Cambridge: Post-War Architecture and the Competition to Build Churchill College* (booklet, Churchill College, 2007).

Architecture: Møller Centre

The architecture of the Møller Centre deserves separate comment. After a limited competition, under the guidance of Sir Colin St John Wilson (Honorary Fellow and architect of the British Library at St Pancras), a design by Henning Larsen (1925-) of Copenhagen was selected. Larsen is chiefly known for his Saudi Foreign Ministry in Riyadh and the Danish Opera House in Copenhagen. The contractor was Johnson and Bailey. The building, with its strong east-west axis, links the main College with the visiting Fellows' and postgraduate apartment blocks beyond. Its heart is the long residential central block, standing three storeys high and just one room in width (the building looks pencil-thin from above); all rooms face south across the playing fields. The east end is terminated by a splayed wall, creating triangular suites. The building is broken near the east end by a wedge driven across its width, with a broad flight of steps. At the west end there are six meeting rooms and a stunning circular staircase encased in glass. Connected to the central spine are three semi-detached 'colonies': at the north-east corner another accommodation suite and at the north-west a lecture theatre seating 95; between these a podium garden; at the south-west corner is an arresting octagonal tower, containing a restaurant, seating 88, lounge bar above, and a rooftop belvedere with a fine view of Cambridge. The tower, faced in white stone, and with a glass pyramid rising above the belvedere, has an almost ecclesiastical appearance, upstaging the modest Chapel that lies beyond. The main building's strong linear spine is traversed by three diagonals: the splayed east end; the wedge; and the entrance walkway which takes visitors from the road and becomes an internal corridor across the main axis to the tower beyond. This walkway and the main axial corridors make for internal 'streets', the latter enlivened by the snaking curvature of the study bedroom walls, and an elegant bridge weaving across the entrance hall at first floor level. The bricks are from the same manufacturer as the College bricks, but of lighter tone. The horizontal banding echoes the College's, but in Portland stone, rather than concrete. The main building has a copper-finished curved roof, echoing the barrel vaults of the College's Dining Hall. However, despite these references to the 'old' College, the Møller Centre looks starkly different, its clinically smooth facades contrasting with Richard Sheppard's highly articulated facades and textural surfaces. The interior aesthetic has a cool purity, in white and deep blue. The colour scheme, together with the spiral staircases and occasional portholes, are reminiscent of an ocean liner, in homage to the nautical source of the Møller Foundation's wealth. The Centre has 71 ensuite bedrooms (60 single, 11 double), including three executive suites; until 1998 27 were used by students, before being transferred for the Centre's exclusive use. In 1993, and again in 2007, the Centre's facilities were enhanced by the building of the adjacent Study Centre, described in Part II.

West Cambridge

When the College began, it was on the outskirts of Cambridge. Only in a bicycle- and pedestrian-dominated town could a college one mile from the Market Square be considered 'a long way out'. Over the past half-century, however, the University's centre of gravity has moved westward. West Cambridge not only has five neighbouring colleges 'on the hill' – Churchill, Fitzwilliam, Lucy Cavendish, Murray Edwards (formerly New Hall), and St Edmund's, but is also the site of the University's principal development zone. Westward, along the Madingley Road, toward the M11 motorway, new science departments have been built, and, during the coming quarter-century, the University intends to develop a large area north-west of the College, toward Girton, for collegiate, research, and residential use.

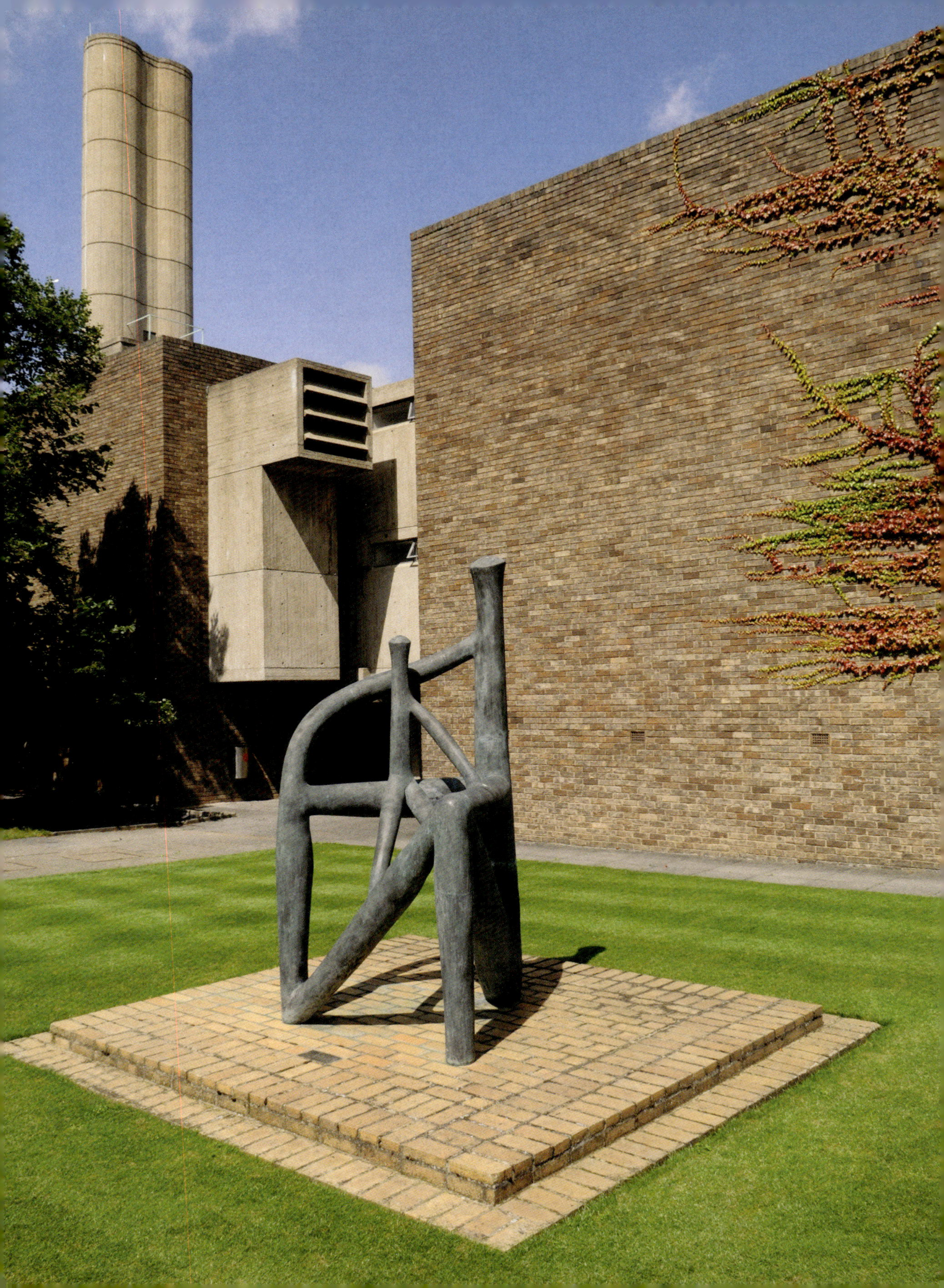

GUIDE TO THE FABRIC

This section provides a guide to the buildings, fabric, and artworks, and to the people associated with them. Only artworks on continuous display are mentioned.

THE SITE. The main site is 42 acres (17 hectares), the largest consolidated site of any Cambridge college. In the Middle Ages, this was part of Grithow Field, monastic land, open until *c.*1800, when St John's College, the post-Reformation landowner, instigated enclosure. It remained farmland until purchased by Churchill College in 1959. Appropriately for a technological college, the world's earliest wireless transmissions were beamed across the site in the 1890s by Lord Rutherford from the adjacent University Observatory to the Cavendish Laboratory in the City centre. Site dimensions: east-west, 590 m. (650 yds); north-south, 230 m. (250 yds) at the eastern boundary (Storey's Way), 340 m. (370 yds) at the western boundary.

ENTRANCE. The College is entered by a concrete-balustraded bridge over a pond, gesturing toward a moat and drawbridge, symbols enforced by the shocking fact, for 1960, that this College had no enclosing walls. In those days, colleges were *in loco parentis* and students subject to strict 'gate hours', confining them at night. The architect originally planned a near-encircling moat.

LEFT: Dhruva Mistry's sculpture sits aptly in front of the architect's essay in expressionist concrete

North side of the entrance court: the sheer brick wall of the squash courts. North-west corner: boilerhouse chimney stack and ventilation louvres, a stunning essay in sculptural concrete 'brutalism', characteristic of the 1960s. Here the symbolism (the chimney has a graceful double-ovoid shape) points firmly to a college for a technological age, eschewing dreaming spires. The space between the boilerhouse and Porters' Lodge was intended for the Chapel, which, after a notorious controversy in 1961, was banished to the site's farthest end. The Chapel roof's low vault would have mirrored the Dining Hall's high vaults beyond. The visual result is a space dominated by squash rather than religion, with a chimney for a campanile.

North lawn: sculpture in bronze, 'Diagram of an Object (Second State)' (1990), an abstract mother and child, by the Gujarati **Dhruva Mistry**, RA, CBE (1957-), artist in residence 1984-5, purchased 1995, with donations by early 1960s alumni and the Tolkien Foundation; another copy at the Hunterian Museum, Glasgow; the College has three works by Mistry. (For many years there stood here a sculpture by **Henry Moore** (1898-1986), 'Three-piece Reclining Figure' (1961-2), recalled by the Moore Foundation, 1988.) South lawn: sculpture in stainless steel, 'Beast Alerted I' (1990) by **Lynn Chadwick** (1914-2003), previously exhibited at Tate Britain.

In search of monumentality, the architect provided the entrance with imposing brick pylons. As in ancient colleges, the entrance is guarded by a **Porters' Lodge**, the College's hub. There is a dramatically novel

The entrance: Richard Sheppard's update of a medieval gatehouse

interpretation of an entrance gate (1964), seven-bar, aluminium, which rotates on its axis, by **Geoffrey Clarke**, RA (1924-), given by the British Aluminium Company. Clarke's best-known decorative metalwork work is at Coventry Cathedral. The student mail room opposite the Porters' Lodge was once filled with telephone switching gear. The adjacent staircase leads to administrative offices; painting: 'Study of the Human Body' (2003) by **Richard Swift**.

Outer wall of the Lodge: a plaque, with the arms of the College and Prince Philip, the College's Visitor, and a motto: *Felix qui potuit rerum cognoscere causas. 5 June 1964* ('Fortunate is he who understands the causes of things'); from Virgil, *Georgics*, ii.490, echoing Lucretius's *De rerum natura* (*On the Nature of Things*), a philosophical poem on the materialist and atomistic philosophies of Epicurus and Democritus. In quoting a Latin poet's hymn to the natural world, the plaque represents a marriage between the sciences and the humanities. (Compare the similar but theistic motto, also in Latin, above the old Cavendish Laboratory: 'Great are the works of the Lord; they are pondered by all who delight in them': Psalm 111).

CONCOURSE. Proceeding from the Porters' Lodge, the sense of entering a Great Court is compromised by the dominating spine of the Concourse straight ahead. Did the architect intend people to experience a courtyard or a street? The walkway to the left leads to residential courtyards, the vista opening on to the Great Court, with the Library and Archives Centre glimpsed beyond. To the right, a small courtyard, with the Dining Hall wall looming above. On the far side of this court, Housekeeper's workrooms; beyond them, Maintenance workshops, loading-bay, staff car parks; above, finance offices (originally nurse's surgery and sick bay). First floor, the **Club Room**, for meetings and dinners: wood (teak) for panelling and floor, given by the Government of India. The stairway offers a striking instance of concrete 'brutalism': ample 'shuttered' concrete showing wood grain effect. Above stairway: a rubbing of one of England's largest brasses, from St Margaret's Church, King's Lynn, given by Richard Keynes (1965): *Robert Braunche d.1364 and his wives.*

Straight ahead from the Lodge, the full length of the brick-floored Concourse is 69 m. (225 ft). Originally unenclosed and windswept for two-thirds of its length; remodelled, 1985, by installation of windows and alcoves to the north, offices to the south, principally for the Tutors for Advanced Students. Alcoves: prints (1922-35) by **Federico Garcia Lorca** (1899-1936), Spanish poet and artist, murdered by fascists; given by M. Vallmitjana, 1982.

FOYER. The Concourse opens on to the Foyer, the College's chief junction. Left: grand staircase to the Dining Hall. Right: Buttery. Ahead: student common rooms. By Buttery entrance, foundation stone, cast in concrete by **Edward Wright** (1912-88), designer and typographer, best-known for his revolving sign at New Scotland Yard, London. Its inscription reads: *This stone was laid on the 14th October 1961 by Lord Tedder GCB, the Chancellor of the University.* Illustrated in Tanya Harrod, *The Crafts in Britain in the Twentieth Century* (1999). An alternative stone, with Churchill's name, was broken up: owing to ill-health the Founder was unable to attend. **Arthur Tedder** (1890-1967) was a founder Trustee, commander of the Royal Air Force during the Second World War, and deputy Supreme Allied Commander under Dwight Eisenhower for the invasion of Europe. Print at Foyer entrance: 'Alan Turing: the Enigma' (2000), from a set of eight, by **Sir Edward Paolozzi**, RA (1924-2005), celebrating the wartime decoder and computing pioneer, with quotations from Andrew Hodges's biography; the other seven are in the Seminar Room (below).

STUDENT COMMON ROOMS. Four common rooms (or 'combination rooms' in Cambridge parlance). Originally three: Middle (postgraduate) Common Room to left, TV room to right, and Quiet Room beyond. Today: games room to left, television room to right, quiet room, and computer room beyond, the latter two with attractive vistas across the playing fields. Games Room: mansonia wood panelling and sapele flooring, given by the Government of Nigeria. Quiet Room: afrormosia wood panelling and sapele flooring, given by the Government of Ghana.

BUTTERY. The College bar: 'buttery' in Cambridge terminology. Originally, a somewhat arid 'airport lounge',

and one in which Fellows, on their way to their common room, risked being skewered by snooker cues: the architect intended Fellows and students to mingle. Remodelled, 1991, by **Geoffrey Spyer**, to a scheme proposed by Fellow in Architecture Marcial Echenique: extended southward toward the Foyer by replacing a fixed glass wall with a sliding partition; extended westward, creating a separate corridor for Fellows; most of the floor area raised to the level of the bar area, creating a partitioned lounge. Through the windows, the Fellows' Garden, used for summer parties. Panelling: British Columbian pine. Brass trophy, 'Madonna and Child' by **Arthur Dooley** (1929-94), presented by Granada Television to the College team which won the national University Challenge quiz tournament in 1970; Dooley is Liverpool's favourite sculptor, a passionate Communist who began as a shipyard welder. Prints,

The foundation stone, cast in concrete – detail

The buttery – Cambridgespeak for the bar

'Cityscapes' (2002), by **Andrew Turnbull**. Above the bar, an oar: *Churchill College Ladies 1st May Boat 1990: Head of the River*, marking the most recent occasion a College boat was Head of the River in the 'Bumps' (the races on the Cam). Painting at end of Fellows' corridor: 'Aux flancs du roc, coup d'aile' (1991) by **Marcel Barbeau** (1925-).

Fellows' rooms and Master's Lodge by keyholder access only. If you do not have access, return to the Foyer and take the Main Staircase: see p. 37.

FELLOWS' GALLERY. Beyond the Buttery, the Fellows' rooms. First, the Fellows' Gallery: renamed thus, 1992, the corridor remodelled and widened by **David Thurlow**, OBE. Left: Senior Common Room, and stairs to the Fellows' Dining Room and Dining Hall. Right: entrance to Wine Cellar (in fact above ground): the Cellar holds wines for College dinners and for sale to Fellows; many of the better wines are bought *en primeur* and left to develop in the Cellar for 10-15 years; hence, the stock is four or five times the annual consumption rate of *c*.6,000 bottles. Far end, left: Cockcroft Room; right: stairs to Fellows' Guest Rooms (in the latter, timber for furniture given by the Government of Jamaica). Paintings and prints: left: 'Blue Incantation' (1999) by **Alan Davie** (1920-); 'August Light, Isle of Man' (1997) by **Julia Ball**; right: '13/12/66' (1966) by **John Hoyland** (1934-), on temporary loan; midway, left and right: 'The Cleric' and 'Psyche' (2001) by **Gary Hume**, RA (1962-); far left: four prints, 'Nineteen Greys', (1968) by **Bridget Riley**, CBE (1931-); far right: eight photographic prints, 'Graffiti' (2004) by **Walter Gilbert** (1932-), Nobel Laureate in Chemistry, donated 2006; end wall: 'Tabard' (1992) by **Albert Irvin**, RA (b.1922), on temporary loan. Bronze statue: 'Une jeune fille' (1963) by **Ernest Wijnants** (1878-1964), given by the Government of Belgium, 1964. Stairwell: sculptures: 'Magus I' and 'Magus II' (1995) by **Jenny Eadon**; painting: 'Three Secrets' (2005) by **Donald Stubbs**.

SENIOR COMMON ROOM. Panelling: Tasmanian oak, tallow wood floor, given by the Government of Australia. One of just two fireplaces in the College, the other in the Master's Lodge. Originally the west end a separate Fellows' Writing Room, nicknamed 'the plotting room'; wall removed, 1977. Furniture by **Robin Day** (1915-): 'Club Armchair' (low and square, black leather on a teak base, very 1960s); 'Plus Table' (coffee tables in African walnut with black vinyl tops); and 'Interplan Desk' (afrormosia frame, black vinyl top); all 1962; exhibited at the Robin and Lucienne Day retrospective, 2001, Barbican Art Gallery. 18th-century corner sideboard, given by Brendan Bracken. Paintings: west wall: print of the Dining Hall (1974) by **Valerie Thornton** (1931-91); 'Over the Sea' (1980) by **Nan Youngman** (1906-95); 'The Avenue' (1903) by French pointillist **Maximilien Luce** (1858-1941), given by Bracken; north wall: 'Crowd Scene' (1990) by **Thomas Newbolt** (1951-), given by Richard Keynes, 1995; east wall: untitled print (1998) by **Marcel Barbeau** (1925-); 'Blue and Green Abstract' by **Alistair Grant** (1925-97). Fireplace: bronze sculpture, 'Monsieur Ingres', by French expressionist **Émile Bourdelle** (1861-1929) (there is a Musée Bourdelle in Paris); Ghanaian wood carving, man and woman embracing.

COCKCROFT ROOM. A dining room and sitting room, with folding partition between, adjunct to the Master's Lodge, shared between the Master and Fellows, originally the 'Guest Dining and Reception Rooms' and the latter fitted out as a library; later named after the first Master.

Sir John Cockcroft (1897-1967), FRS, KCB, OM, Nobel Prize in Physics (1951), for splitting the atom, with Ernest Walton, at the Cavendish Lab in 1932. Educated at Manchester and Cambridge Universities; directed wartime atomic research in Canada, then Atomic Energy Research Establishment at Harwell, 1946-58; first Master of Churchill, 1959-67; Chancellor, Australian National University, 1961-5. See C. P. Snow, *The New Men* (1954); Guy Hartcup and T. E. Allibone, *Cockcroft and the Atom* (1984); Brian Cathcart, *The Fly in the Cathedral* (2004).

The Senior Common Room

The architect had a knack for rapid translation from concrete brutalism to demure wood panelling; this room could be in one of the 'old' colleges. Rimu wood, given by the (then) 'Dominion' of New Zealand; teak flooring, given by the 'Dominion' of Trinidad and Tobago. Dining room: bronze bust of Sir John Cockcroft (1970) by the Russian **Nikolai Nikogosian** (1918-), given by the artist, 1989; drawing of Lady (Elizabeth) Cockcroft (1962) by **Robert Tollast** (d.2008); painting by **Winston Churchill**, 'Orchids' (1948), illustrated in Churchill's *Painting as a Pastime* (1950); several pictures from the Maisonneuve Collection, including two prints by **Henri Toulouse Lautrec** (1864-1901): 'La Châtelaine' ('The Lady of the Manor', 1895) and 'Marcelle Linder' (1895). Sitting room, another painting by **Churchill**, 'The Atlantic, near Biarritz' (1931), given by Bracken. For Churchill's paintings see Minnie Churchill and David Coombs, *Sir Winston Churchill's Life Through his Paintings* (2004). Print (1990) by **Peter Lyon** of a pencil drawing of sculptor Henry Moore (1923) by **Robert Lyon** (1894-1978), the first known likeness, done when both were students at the Royal College of Art; another in the National Portrait Gallery. A pair of wine cabinets, given by Bracken. Note bellpushes for summoning waiters, long disused, echoing an older, grander collegiate lifestyle.

MASTER'S LODGE. A private house set within the College, protected by small enclosed patios, the design irregular; four bedrooms, originally more before remodelling. The College's modernity notwithstanding, the kitchen has a set of servants' bells, and the first floor originally had a flat for a resident housekeeper, now providing two bedrooms. Some of the Lodge's furniture belonged to Brendan Bracken, mostly 19th-century copies of 18th-century models. The dining room (originally the Master's study) perhaps the most elegant room in the College: satinwood panelling given by the Government of Ceylon (Sri Lanka); wheelback and ribbonback chairs and occasional tables; painting of Edmund Burke, Whig statesman and philosopher (once vaunted by the Conservative Party), attributed to **George Romney** (1734-1802); from the Bracken estate, a prized possession which hung at his home, 8 Lord North Street, London, gazing upon visiting Tory grandees; briefly stolen for ransom by his impecunious brother. Drawing room: two Ghanaian (Ashanti) chiefs' stools, the king's with vertical supports, the queen's with circular, given by Joseph and Mrs Quartey; graphite drawing of **C. P. Snow** (1963) by **Michael Ayrton** (1921-75), given by George Steiner; ceramic sculpture, 'Blue Woman' (c.1990) by **Trupti Patel** (1957-); bronze centenary sculpture of Churchill (1974), by **Karin Churchill**, given by the artist. Table in entrance hall, 'Capillary' (1996) by **Gareth Neal** (1974-).

FELLOWS' DINING ROOM. From the Fellows' Gallery a staircase leads to the Fellows' Dining Room and Dining Hall. Portraits of the first five masters: Sir John Cockcroft (1962) by **Robert Tollast** (d.2008); Sir William Hawthorne (1984) by **Rodrigo Moynihan**, RA (1910-90); Sir Hermann Bondi (1989) by **June Mendoza**; Sir Alec Broers (1996) by **Jason Sullivan**; Sir John Boyd (2008) by **Tom Phillips**, RA (1937-). In the background of the last, Lady (Julia) Boyd; the Taoist adage bears several possible readings, including 'Govern, avoiding unnecessary intervention'; the sitter himself prefers 'Go with the flow'. Upper landing: sculpture in wood, 'Zelah' (1961) by **Denis Mitchell** (1912-93), given by his widow, 1997. The Fellows' Dining Room, which can dine up to 60, also used for Governing Body and Council meetings. Black bean wood panelling and tallow wood flooring, given by the Government of Australia. Two carpets given by the Government of Pakistan. At dinner the presiding Fellow may sit in Winston Churchill's chair, presented to his father Lord Randolph Churchill by King Edward VII when Prince of Wales, on loan from Mr Winston Churchill; note the Prince's *fleurs de lis*. Bronze bust of Churchill by **Jacob Epstein** (1880-1959), presented by Lord Thomson of Fleet and *The Sunday Times*, 1966; one of several copies cast in the 1940s; in 2001 the British Government loaned one to President George W. Bush for the White House; others at the National Portrait Gallery, Imperial War Museum, and Churchill Museum, Fulton, Missouri. North wall: two paintings by **John Hoyland** (1934-), on temporary loan. East wall: 'Expulsion of Pain' (2002-6) by **Dhruva Mistry**, RA, CBE (1957-), an interpretation of Picasso's

The Master's Lodge

'Guernica' (1937); the original was Picasso's protest against war, depicting the Fascist aerial bombardment of the Basque town during the Spanish Civil War. West wall: 10 silkscreen prints, 'Marilyn Monroe' (1962, the year of her suicide), by the American Pop artist **Andy Warhol** (1928-87), on temporary loan; Colin Fraser, chair of the College's Hanging Committee, remarks: 'In what other Cambridge college would you find Marilyn Monroe adorning the walls of the Fellows' dining room?'

Enter the Dining Hall (see below); or return to the ground floor, and retrace steps through the Buttery to the Foyer.

MAIN STAIRCASE, MEZZANINE, DINING HALL FOYER. From the Foyer, a majestic 6.7 m. (22 ft) flight of stairs to the Dining Hall. A large bronze bust of Churchill (1961) by **Oscar Nemon**, donated by the British Government, 1963: Winston stern and determined, supported by a suitably craggy concrete bracket; other copies at Windsor Castle, Chartwell, Blenheim Palace, Conservative Party headquarters in Smith Square, the Australian Parliament building in Canberra, and Winston Churchill Park in Copenhagen.

Oscar Nemon (1906-85), born in the Austro-Hungarian empire; settled in Brussels, lodging with Magritte; found refuge in England, 1939; his mother and grandmother killed in Auschwitz. After the War, sculptor to the 'great and good': busts of the Queen, Queen Mother, President Eisenhower, and Prime Ministers Macmillan and Thatcher. Nemon met Churchill at Marrakesh, 1951, became firm friends, and sculpted him at least eight times; these include the full-length Winston, brooding and overcoated, standing in Parliament Square; and another in the Palace of Westminster, touched for luck by MPs passing into the Commons. See www.oscarnemon.org.uk.

Playwright **Wole Soyinka** (1934-) recalls that, when a visiting Fellow in 1973, he came down the stairs past the bust of Churchill, 'the great colonialist', and

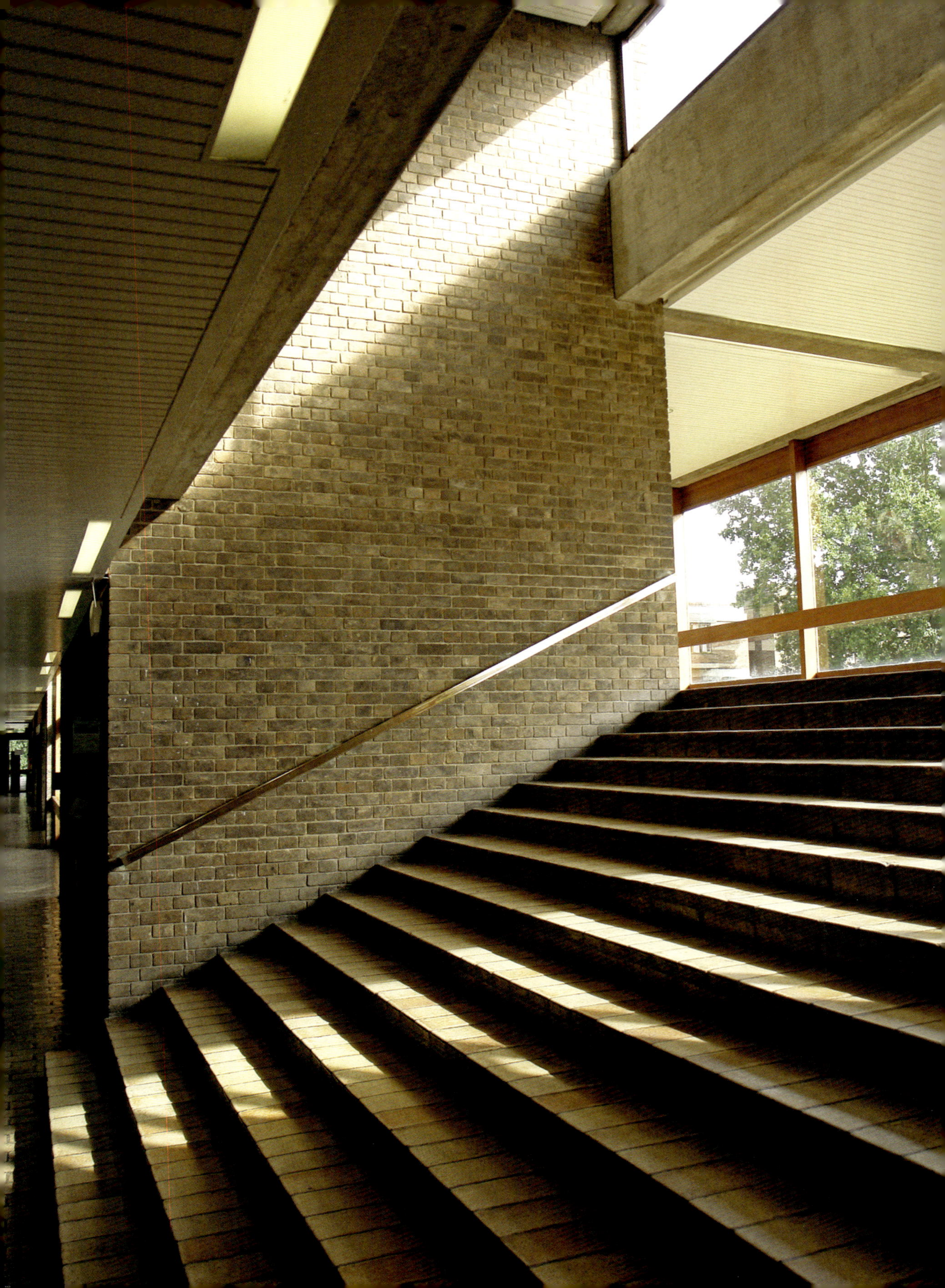

Oscar Nemon's bust of Winston Churchill

was tempted to topple it with an 'accidental push'; instead, he wrote his play *Death and the King's Horseman*, a tragedy set in Nigeria in 1946, singled out for mention when Soyinka became the first African to win the Nobel Prize for Literature.

On the mezzanine, two small sculptures, 'Euclid and Chaos' (1989) by **Martin Rodda**, and 'Mourning Woman' (1993) by **Daphne Hardy Henrion** (1917-2003). Henrion's remarkable life included a wartime love affair with Arthur Koestler; she smuggled the manuscript of his *Darkness at Noon* out of Nazi-occupied France. From the mezzanine a panorama of the College: left, residential courtyards; centre, the Library; right, playing fields, the Chapel in the distance.

Dining Hall Foyer. Right: a void with balcony overlooking Concourse below; infilled, 1988, for use as a computer room; discontinued and re-opened, 2007, now with disabled lift. Left, void infilled, 1988, for an office. Right: bronze sculpture, a Sokoke Scops Owl by **Louisa Forbes** (1962-), in memory of Andrew Batchelor (d.1992), who died while an undergraduate; certificate recording a star named for David Gunn (d.1998), who died shortly after graduating.

TIZARD AND ASHMORE ROOMS. At west end of the Hall Foyer, left, the **Tizard Room**, a meeting room, named in 2006, formerly the Small Combination Room, and originally the Women's Common Room (a daring innovation in 1964).

Richard (Dick) Tizard (1917-2005), engineer, founder Fellow, second Senior Tutor. Son of leading wartime scientist Sir Henry Tizard; educated at Oxford University; worked in aerial defence research during the War, helping design gyroscopic gun sights; scientific researcher at the National Physical Laboratory, in industry, and London School of Economics, 1947-61; founder member of the

LEFT: The principal staircase

British Computer Society; joined Churchill College, 1960, and devoted himself to teaching, tutoring, and college governance; led campaign for admission of women and pioneered broadened access in undergraduate admissions from state schools. A keen yachtsman, he features, in youth, in letters of Arthur Ransome: an original Swallow or Amazon.

21 drawings (1962-5) of all the founder Trustees (except Sir Winston) and some founder Fellows by **Robert Tollast** (d.2008), given by Sir John Cockcroft. Trustees: Lord Adrian, Lord Annan, William Carron, Lord Chandos, Sir John Colville, Brian Downs, Lord Fleck, Lord Godber, Lord Knollys, Lord Tedder, Lord Todd, Lord Weeks (see Appendix 3). Master and Fellows: Sir John Cockcroft, Philip Ashmore, Sir Edward Bullard, Francis Crick, Alan Katritzky, Richard Keynes, John Morrison, John Oriel, C. P. Snow.

Next to this room, a television room (originally, in 1964, the Junior Common Room). Beyond it, the

'Winston Churchill in 1915' by John Leigh-Pemberton after William Orpen

Sandy Ashmore Room: the Middle Common Room and bar, named in 2006; from which a magnificent view westwards. These rooms: Tasmanian oak panelling.

Philip (Sandy) Ashmore (1916-2002), physical chemist, founder Fellow and first Tutor for Advanced Students, 1960-3. Educated, Cambridge University; Royal Air Force during the War, rising to Squadron Leader; returned to a lectureship in physical chemistry, and Fellowship of Emmanuel College; to Churchill College, 1960; professor, Manchester Institute of Science and Technology, 1963-81; editor of *Combustion and Flame*.

OFFICES. Running eastward from the Hall Foyer, a corridor of administrative offices for the Master, Bursar, Senior Tutor, Admissions Tutors, Development Office, Registrar, and Computer Manager. The easternmost end, above the Porters' Lodge, originally the bursary. Rubber flooring given by the Government of Malaysia, now covered by parquet. Photographs (1996, 2008) by **Julia Hedgecoe** (1938-), of the second to sixth masters (Sir William Hawthorne, Sir Hermann Bondi, Sir Alec Broers, Sir John Boyd, Sir David Wallace), Honorary Fellows (Sir Martin Gilbert, Sir John Gurdon, Lady Mary Soames, Maersk McKinney Møller, Garfield Weston, Lord (Michael) Young, and Njabulo Ndebele; see Appendix 4), and Antony Hewish, Fellow and Nobel Laureate. Bursar's Office: South African stinkwood desk and lion feet chairs, given by the Government of South Africa, 1961; bronze: 'Le Coq Dormant' by **François Pompon** (1855-1933), pupil of Rodin. Senior Tutor's Office: resin copy of bronze head of Churchill.

DINING HALL. Opened 1964; the largest in Cambridge, 22 m. (72 ft) square, its floor area one fifth greater than its nearest rival, Trinity; seats 430; a monument to an era that assumed all students would dine together nightly in 'Formal Hall'; almost as soon built, superseded by the cafeteria age that ensures today's students dine formally only on special occasions; a fine asset, nonetheless, for College feasts, and for the conference business. Standing 9 m. (30 ft) to the base of the vault beams, it is 11.6 m. (38 ft) to the highest point. Overhead, three giant concrete barrel vaults, among the largest in Britain, spanning

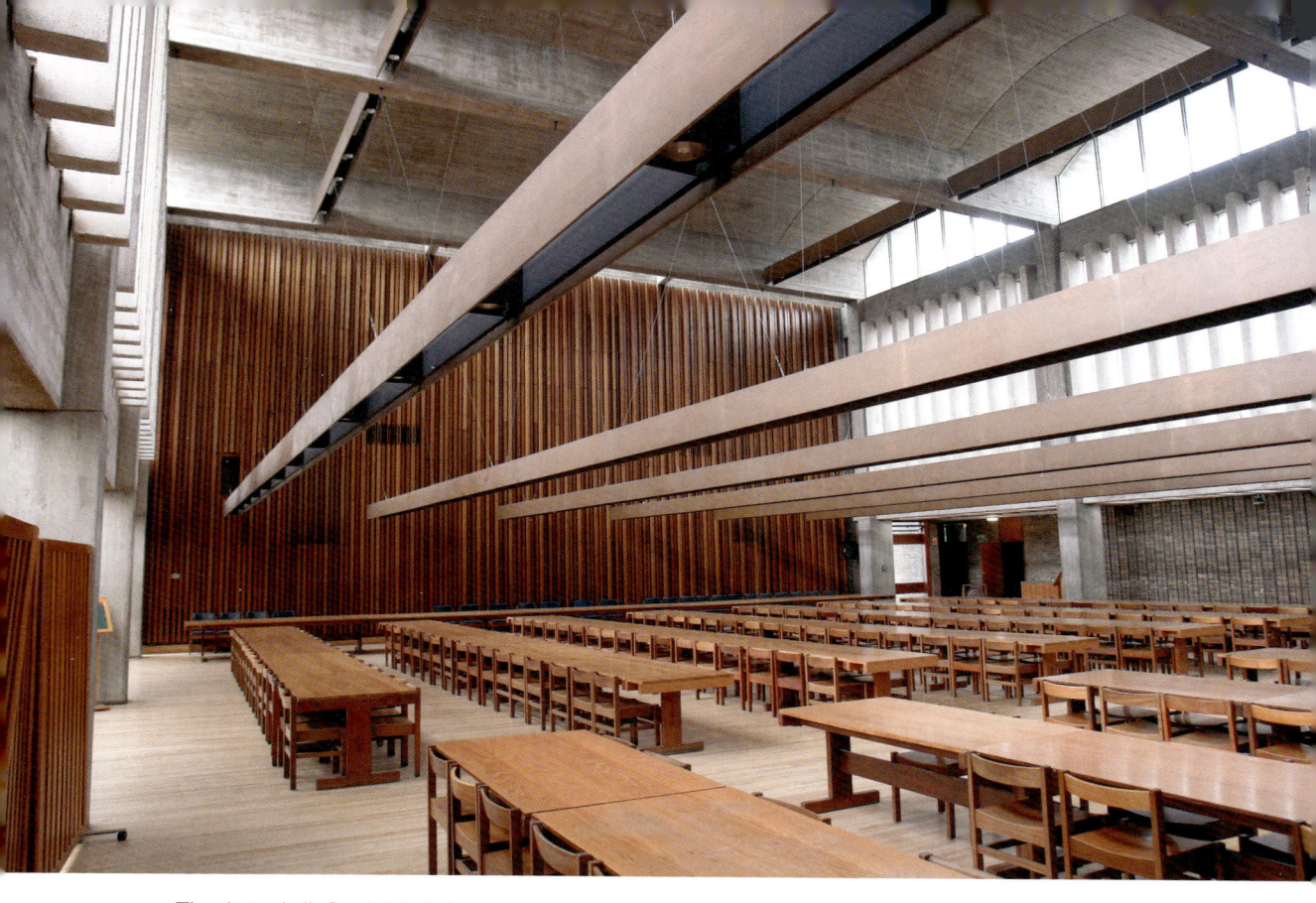

The dining hall, Cambridge's largest

20.4 m. (67 ft), or 23.3 m. (76 ft) including the cantilevered end section. The shells have a rise of 1.2 m. (4 ft) and are 7 m. (23 ft) broad; the valley and edge beams are 1.2 m. (4 ft) deep. The vaults are closed by lunette windows. Sixty soaring concrete mullions in the windows, north and south, each weighing two tons. Low aisles to north and south have fluted brick acoustic walls. Slatted wood panelling (Western red cedar) to east and west walls, from British Columbia, given by the Government of Canada. Birch flooring. Copper for low-slung light fittings (which obstruct the view of the great vault) given by the Government of the Central African Federation (Northern Rhodesia, Southern Rhodesia, Nyasaland: today Zambia, Zimbabwe, Malawi). Chairs and tables in teak designed by **Robin Day** (1915-), commissioned 1962, manufactured by Heals; High Table (not in fact high, there is no dais) and chairs given by Lord Godber (founder Trustee). North-west corner: Fellows' entrance and access to the Fellows' Dining Room.

South wall, the sole portrait: Churchill in 1915, a copy (1962) by **John Leigh-Pemberton** (1911-97) of an original by **Sir William Orpen**, RA (1878-1931), given by the Trustees, 1965. Orpen painted Winston at bay, out of office and humiliated after the Gallipoli disaster; it was Winston's favourite portrait, a warning against hubris.

Returning downstairs to the Foyer, a door beside the Main Staircase leads to a short walkway to the Library, Wolfson Hall, and Archives Centre, the second central block of College buildings, opened in 1965. Straight ahead for the Wolfson Hall and Library; left and around the front of the Library for the Archives Centre.

WOLFSON HALL. Lecture theatre seating 300, named after the philanthropist and Honorary Fellow Sir Isaac Wolfson (who also gives his name to Wolfson College, Churchill's Wolfson Flats, and much else: 'the first man since Jesus Christ to have a college named

The Bracken Reading Room and Jean Lurçat's tapestry

after him at both Oxford and Cambridge'). Wolfson (1897-1991), son of a Jewish cabinet maker, was chairman of Great Universal Stores, 1947-87, and creator of the Wolfson Foundation. The Hall was state-of-the-art for its time, including a simultaneous translation booth which Sir John Cockcroft was anxious to include to stage the international 'Pugwash' (Atoms for Peace) conferences. Foyer: portrait of Wolfson by **Robert Tollast** (d.2008), commissioned by the College, 1965. Eight pictures of College scenes (1992), by **Robert Mason**: 'Art and Architecture', 'Coming and Going under the Watchful Eye of the Head Porter', 'Conference Delegates', 'Conference in Session', 'Henning Larsen's Møller Centre', 'Poster Workshop', 'Conversing', and 'Bicycles'. Plaque commemorating the Royal Institute of British Architects' Award for the best new building in the eastern region of England, 1968. Off the Foyer, Seminar Room: seven prints by **Sir Edward Paolozzi**, RA (1924-2005), 'The Alan Turing Suite' (2000), celebrating the wartime decoder and computing pioneer, with quotations from Andrew Hodges's biography. End of Foyer: **Bevin Room**, with a fine vista.

BRACKEN AND BEVIN LIBRARIES. Accessible to members 24 hours a day, the College library has 48,000 books and 3,500 bound journal volumes, supplementing University departmental libraries and the University Library. Black bean reading desks, by **Robin Day** (1915-), made by Great Universal Stores, 1965. The library is in two parts, the ground floor majestic, the upper floor domestic. Downstairs, the **Bracken Library**, given by his friends. Entrance lobby: portrait of Bracken by **Sir Edwin Lutyens** (1869-1944), given 1966. A book of donors to the Bracken Bequest, and donors' plaque: *A constant lover of the best whose rare qualities of heart and mind they desire to be remembered in this place.*

Brendan Bracken (1901-58), Conservative politician, publisher, wartime propaganda minister. A self-made arriviste; born in Tipperary, fled a Jesuit College and settled in England, 1919. Entered publishing; owned *The Economist*, chairman of the *Financial Times*, founded *History Today*. Faithful and lifelong friend of Churchill, so devoted it was rumoured he was his illegitimate son; at Winston's side throughout the War. MP, 1929-51; Minister of Information, 1941-5; First Lord of the Admiralty, 1945; Viscount Bracken, 1952. The model for Rex Mottram in Evelyn Waugh's *Brideshead Revisited* (1945). The Bracken Bequest included furniture and silver for the Master's use. See Charles Lysaght, *Brendan Bracken* (1979).

The library is a fine space, fenestrated, like the Dining Hall, with multiple slim concrete mullions clad with quartz. Wood (black bean) panelling and shelving given by the Government of Australia. End wall: a magnificent **Lurçat** tapestry, three metres square, 'Etoile de Paris', made at Aubusson, 1948, given by President Charles de Gaulle, 1961. The composition celebrates the liberation of Paris from the Nazis in 1945, the cockerel standing for the defiant spirit of France. The verses at the top are in Provençal dialect. De Gaulle's gift was characteristically backhanded – his relationship with Churchill was fraught: the verses on the left declare, *Paris, soi-meme liberé* ('Paris, *self*-liberated'): on Liberation Day, 1944, he pronounced, 'Paris a été libéré par son peuple'; the American and British armies did indeed allow Free French troops to enter Paris first.

Jean Lurçat (1892-1966), born in the Vosges, wounded at Verdun in the First World War, active in the Resistance in the Second; first exhibited in Paris, 1922; settled in Tours de St Laurent above Saint-Cere, Lot, 1945. His work in oils, theatrical scenery, mosaics, ceramics, lithographs, and tapestry can be seen in the Atelier-Musee Jean Lurçat at Angers. His *Tribute to the Dead of the Resistance* hangs in the National Museum of Modern Art, Paris; his great apocalyptic cycle of the 1950s, in contemplation of nuclear war, *Le Chant du Monde*, hangs at Angers.

Cantilevered Gallery, designed by **Thurlow, Carnell, and Thornburrow**, added 1997. Plaque at top of spiral stairway: *This gallery was constructed with funds generously provided by Sir Emmanuel Kaye CBE, the Sir Edward Lewis Foundation, the A.P. and Chastine McKinney Møller Foundation, the Pearson Charitable Trust, the Lady Soames DBE, Garry Weston DL.*

The upper reading room is reached via a circular top-lit stairway, one of the few curved elements in a rectilinear college. Upper landing: bronze bust (1946) of Ernest Bevin by **Jacob Epstein** (1880-1959): Lady Epstein's copy, purchased by the College, 1967. Photographs of Cuban scenes (1990-4) by **Tony Keeler** (1933-). Sculpture: 'War' (1972) by **Michael Gillespie** (1929-). Librarian's office to left. Right: computer room, turned to this purpose, 1992, named the **Lloyd's Room**, marking a gift by the Lloyd's insurance market, London. The upper library is named the **Bevin Library**, and was funded by the Transport and General Workers' Union.

Ernest Bevin (1881-1951), trade union leader and Labour statesman. Illegitimate child, became a farm worker at 11, and full-time Dockers' Union official, 1911. Led boycott of dispatch of arms for use against the Russian revolutionaries, 1920, but later was a tough anti-Communist. Ruthlessly merged 14 unions into the mighty Transport and General Workers' Union, of which first General Secretary, 1922. Pro-rearmament within the pacifist Labour Party, 1930s. Labour MP, 1940-51; Minister of Labour in Churchill's wartime coalition, 1940-5, brilliantly managing manpower deployment; member of War Cabinet. Foreign Secretary, 1945-51, in Clement Attlee's Labour Government; a chief architect of the North Atlantic Treaty Organisation (NATO), 1949; said to be the British politician Stalin most feared.

Within the Bevin Library, prints, 'Canaveral', by **Dame Barbara Hepworth**, given by Richard Hey, founder Fellow. A sculpture, 'Reguarding Guardian I' (1985), by **Dhruva Mistry**, RA, CBE (1957-), metal and painted plaster, bright red, a winged mythical beast with a human head, and prominent horns, claws, tail, and penis; other versions in Victoria Square, Birmingham, and Pallent House Gallery, Chichester. Far end: a lounge, formerly the Bevin West Room, renamed the **Maisonneuve Room**, 1993, to mark a bequest of artworks.

Karsh's classic image of Winston Churchill, engraved on the door of the Jock Colville Hall

Pierre Maisonneuve (1898-1965), poet and patron of the arts. Settled in London, 1921; prospered in the clothing trade; General de Gaulle's commercial secretary in wartime. Befriended young French painters and sculptors, purchased their works, and ran a gallery. His substantial collection of post-Impressionist paintings given to the College in honour of Winston Churchill.

In this room, stone bust of Maisonneuve (1949), by **Mark Szwarc** (1892-1958); bronze nude, by **Paul Cornet** (1892-1977); bronze dancer and two stone nudes kneeling, by **Hubert Yencesse** (1900-87), pupil of Maillot; bronze 'Three Graces' by **Alfred Auguste Janniot** (1889-1969). Two cabinets of books: part of Maisonneuve's collection of 1,200 classic (mainly 19th century) French literature; and Winston Churchill's collection of Napoleana, 173 titles in 296 volumes (1802-1957), in uniform binding, which stood in his study at Chartwell, donated by Clementine Churchill, 1965. She also gave the Library copies of de Gaulle's speeches inscribed by the General.

Unlike ancient colleges, Churchill has no additional inner or Old Library of rare and antiquarian books. There are, however, a couple of further special collections: the John Cowper Powys collection of first editions of his novels, and Stephen Roskill's history collection, held in the Roskill Library (below). The library possesses a first edition of **Isaac Newton's** *Opticks* (1704).

ARCHIVES CENTRE. Opened in 1973 by US ambassador Walter Annenberg in the presence of HRH the Duke of Edinburgh and Lady Spencer-Churchill; the final part of the original College buildings. Entered via the **Jock Colville Hall**, named 1989, formerly the Exhibition Hall. North wall: slate plaque by **David Kindersley** (1915-95), Cambridge's best-known letter cutter, pupil of Eric Gill: *The Jock Colville Hall named in recognition of Sir John Colville CB CVO 1915-1987, diplomat, banker, writer. Principal Private Secretary to Sir Winston Churchill. Honorary Fellow of the College. For his services to the foundation and life of Churchill College.*

Sir John (Jock) Colville (1915-87), CB, CVO, secretary to Churchill, 1940-1, 1943-5, 1951-5. Grandson of a marquess and a viscount and nephew of a duchess, Colville lived at the heart of the Establishment; page to King George V; educated at Cambridge; civil servant; secretary to Princess Elizabeth, 1947-9; later a banker; a creator of Churchill College; Honorary Fellow. His Downing Street diaries, *The Fringes of Power* (1985), arguably provide the best insight into Churchill in wartime; autobiographical essays: *Footprints in Time* (1976).

Beneath, bronze relief commemorating the Gallipoli (Dardanelles) campaign, of which Churchill was a leading advocate, showing the Anzac (Australian and New Zealand Army Corps) battlefield, 1915, and location of war memorials; on loan from the Palace of Westminster, courtesy of Sir Robert Rhodes James (1933-99), historian, MP for Cambridge. The main doors, 1971, bronze, designed by **Geoffrey Clarke**, RA (1924-). Right door: Churchill's image, engraved from the most famous of all images of Winston, taken Ottawa, 1941, by Armenian-born Canadian photographer **Yousuf Karsh** (1908-2002). It is said Karsh achieved Winston's classic bulldog pose by snatching his cigar a moment before taking the shot. It made Karsh's career, symbolising a Britain defiant and unconquerable. See Karsh, *Faces of Destiny* (1947); Maria Tippett, *Portrait in Light and Shadow* (2008). Left door: Churchill's arms with family motto, *Fiel pero desdichado* ('Faithful but unfortunate'). Inscription on threshold: *These bronze doors are a gift of a few of the North American Producers of Non-Ferrous Metals as symbols of their enduring admiration for Sir Winston Churchill: American Metal Climax; American Smelting & Refining; Anaconda; International Nickel; Kennecott; Newmont; Phelps Dodge; Designer Geoffrey Clarke ARA; Constructed by Grundy Arnatt Limited.* By the entrance, plan of the British Navy's disposition at the Spithead Review, 28 June 1977, for the Queen's Silver Jubilee, presented by nuclear-powered submarine HMS Churchill. South wall: bronze lettering records the benefactors who paid for the Centre, including all United States ambassadors to Britain, 1925-73, or their descendants (dates are ambassadorial tenures):

Barbara Hepworth's 'Four Square Walk Through': the College's most beloved sculpture

This Archives Centre was built and endowed by and in memory of these United States Ambassadors to the Court of St James's and other eminent Americans, as a tribute to the importance and leadership of Sir Winston Churchill, at once a British subject and an honorary American citizen. Winthrop W. Aldrich 1953-57. Henry J. Heinz II. Walter H. Annenberg 1969-74. Alanson Houghton 1925-29. Vincent Astor. Joseph P. Kennedy 1938-40. Robert W. Bingham 1933-37. John L. Loeb. David K. F. Bruce 1961-69. Andrew M. Mellon 1932-33. Lewis W. Douglas 1947-50. David Rockefeller. Henry Ford II. Thomas J. Watson Jr. Maxwell M. Geffen. John Hay Whitney 1957-61. Walter S. Gifford 1950-53. John G. Winant 1941-46. W. Averell Harriman 1946-47.

The Hall has a standing exhibition introducing the College and Archives Centre. Display includes film showing Winston Churchill speaking at the College site, 17 October 1959. Also, print of a popular wartime painting of Churchill, 1942, by the Hungarian **Arthur Pan** (*fl.*1920-60), source of the most readily available poster of him; this one hung in the Winston Churchill pub on Madingley Road opposite the College until its closure in 1998. Stairs lead to the Search Rooms (lift installed, 2002). Half-landing: benefactors board, 1992 and later:

Garfield Weston Foundation; Mary W. Harriman Foundation; Anglia Television Group plc; Esmée Fairbairn Charitable Trust; Josephine and John J. Louis Fund; Annenberg Foundation; Wolfson Foundation; Isaac Newton Trust; Leverhulme Trust; Daily Telegraph plc; Fairleigh S. Dickinson Jr Foundation Inc.; Dulverton Trust; Heritage Lottery Fund; J. Paul Getty KBE; Cable and Wireless plc; Medlock Charitable Trust; Coca Cola Great Britain; Rank Foundation; Clothworkers' Foundation; Ronald Gerard OBE; Bay Foundation; Ian Rushbrook Esq.

The Search Rooms were formerly approached by a gallery open to the Hall below; these rooms for researchers were enlarged, 1996, incorporating the gallery. They contain a reference library of 5000 books on 20th-century history, and terminals for searching catalogues. The larger room is the **Roskill Library**.

Stephen Roskill (1903-82), CBE, DSC, FBA, naval officer and historian. Educated at Osborne and Dartmouth Royal Naval colleges; served at sea, 1920s-30s; Admiralty staff, 1939; captain, 1944; chief British observer, Bikini Atoll atomic bomb tests, 1946. Self-taught historian, his 10 books include the official naval history of the Second World War, *The War at Sea* (1954-60). Fellow of Churchill College, 1961-82, the only Fellow to have no university degree (besides, later, honorary degrees). Since 1985 the Roskill family has sponsored the biennial Roskill Memorial Lecture. See Barry Gough, *Writing and Fighting Naval History* (2011).

In the Roskill Library, a bust of Churchill (1970) by Czech-born **Franta Belsky** (1921-2000), given by the artist; copies also at Fulton, Missouri, and the Churchill Hotel, Portman Square, London; another Churchill bust by Belsky was erected in Prague shortly after the fall of the Communist regime; Belsky was twice exiled, by the Nazis in 1939 and the Communists in 1948. Drawing of Stephen Roskill (1978) by **Michael Noakes** (1933-). A small display of Churchilliana and facsimiles of key documents from the archives. The windows record donors to the Capital Campaign, 2004-7, which secured financial independence for the Centre, previously grant-aided by the College:

HRH Prince Bandar bin Sultan bin Abdul Aziz; Annenberg Foundation; Garfield Weston Foundation; Winston Churchill Foundation of the United States; Mr Facundo and Mrs Elizabeth Bacardi; Mr Salvatore and Mrs Alison Bommarito; Mr Donald L. Bryant Jr; Mr Douglas N. and Mrs Delphine H. Daft; Mr Alfred C. Eckert III; Mr David A. and Mrs Kyoko Gledhill; Mr Robert Hamwee; Mr and Mrs Charles Harris; Mr William B. and Mrs Sandra Johnson; Kapnick Foundation; Mrs Sherri Parker Lee; Mr Willem and Mrs Lisa Mesdag; Mr Jerold J. Principato MD; Mr Elihu and Mrs Susan Rose; Satter Foundation; Howard and Debbie Schiller Foundation; Dr and Mrs Monroe E. Trout; Mr Anthony W. Wild.

The Archives Centre Extension (left), built to house Margaret Thatcher's papers

The smaller Search Room named, 2000, the **Harold W. Siebens Reading Room**, in honour of a benefaction. Siebens (1906-89), a native of Storm Lake, Iowa, was an oilman and philanthropist, and an admirer of Lady Thatcher.

Beyond the Roskill Library and a 12 cm thick steel door, the strongrooms (strictly closed to visitors); the original strongroom, on a single floor, and the Extension of 2002, on four floors, which increased storage capacity threefold (from 2,250 to 6,750 linear metres of shelving); between them they can store 67,000 archive boxes; temperature and humidity controlled for optimum preservation conditions; gas fire suppression system. Displayed in the Extension, three tattered flags, two British, one Argentinean, flown

'Three figures' by Sean Crampton

on South Georgia Island during the Falklands War, 1982; donated by Capt. Nicholas Barker, whose pre-war warnings from HMS Endurance of Argentinean activity went unheeded by the British Government; display case gift of Ronald Gerard.

Top floor: Conservation Workshop. Ground floor: the Centre's offices. Staircase from reading rooms to offices: portrait, 1953, of **Sir Barnes Wallis** (1887-1986), by **Alfred Egerton Cooper** (1883-1974); an earlier version is in the National Portrait Gallery. Wallis was an aircraft engineer and inventor, designer of the R100 airship, inventor of geodetic construction and variable geometry aircraft, and the bouncing bomb, immortalised in the 1954 film *The Dam Busters*. Quotation from Horace, *Odes*, 2.21-4: *Virtus, recludens immeritis mori; / caelum, negata temptat iter via, / coetusque vulgaris et udam / spernit humum fugiento penna* (approximately: 'Virtue, which opens the heavens to those who deserve not to die, opens a path denied to the masses, and soars to the firmament'). For an unusual introduction to mathematics see Mary Stopes-Roe (ed.), *Maths with Love: The Courtship Correspondence of Barnes Wallis, Inventor of the Bouncing Bomb* (2005).

In the Great Court, the exterior of the Extension is inscribed (letters cut by the **Cardozo Kindersley Workshop**):

The new wing of the Churchill Archives Centre was built with the generous support of Baroness Thatcher to house her papers. It was endowed by the Margaret Thatcher Foundation; HRH Prince Bandar bin Sultan bin Abdul Aziz; British Petroleum plc; Clore Duffield Foundation; Jean Duffield; Dr Young-Fa Chang; Evergreen Group; Sir Paul Getty KBE; Hobson Charity Ltd; Eric Hotung; Sir K. S. Li and Hutchison Whampoa; Jupiter Asset Management; David W. Packard; Rudolph Palumbo Charitable Foundation; Josie and Julian Robertson; Wafic Rida Said; Harold W. Siebens; Sunley Foundation; Charles Wolfson Charitable Trust; Wolfson Foundation; Mr and Mrs Charles Wyly. 'The inheritance bequeathed to us by former wise or valiant men becomes a rich estate to be enjoyed and used by all' – Sir Winston Churchill.

One of the ten residential courtyards

'Spiral' by Michael Gillespie

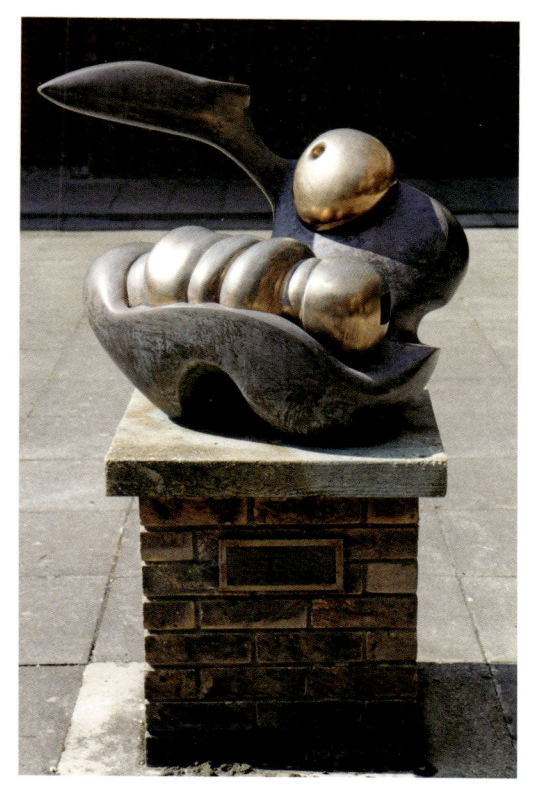

'Pointing figure with child' by Bernard Meadows

The Churchill quotation is from a speech at Bristol University, 2 July 1938. The Extension, by **David Thurlow, Carnell, and Curtis** (2001-2) subtly interjects into Sheppard's courtyard, despite its four-storey scale, with only its projecting glass 'butterfly wings' denoting its more recent provenance. It was opened by former Prime Minister Margaret Thatcher, whose papers are the Centre's second largest collection, and who led the appeal to fund the building.

GREAT COURT (or MAIN COURT): the central lawns, enclosed by the residential courtyards and bisected by the Library and Archives Centre. East side: near the Porters' Lodge, by Staircase 31, oak tree (*Quercus Robur*) planted by Winston Churchill on his only visit, 17 October 1959, before anything was built. He also planted the close-by black mulberry (*Morus Nigra*), East Court by Staircase 31, now recumbent but thriving. Also nearby, beside the Concourse, a weeping mulberry (*Morus Alba*), planted 17 October 2009, by Churchill's daughter, Lady Mary Soames.

South-east corner: bronze sculpture, 'Three Figures', 1970, by **Sean Crampton** (1918-99). In front of the Archives Centre, a bronze sculpture, 'Flight', 1981, by **Peter Lyon** (d.2001), given by Stephen and Mrs Elizabeth Roskill, 1981. West of the central buildings, a sculpture, Cornish granite, 'To Boullée', 1993, by **Michael Dan Archer** (1955-), a homage to the visionary French neoclassical architect Étienne-Louis Boullée: the latter's unbuilt project for a domical Cenotaph for Isaac Newton (1784) is echoed.

Further west, a large bronze sculpture, standing 4.3 m. (14 ft) high, 'Four Square Walk Through' (1966) by **Dame Barbara Hepworth**, loaned, 1968, by the sculptor, on permanent loan from the Fitzwilliam Museum since 1999. Another copy at the Barbara

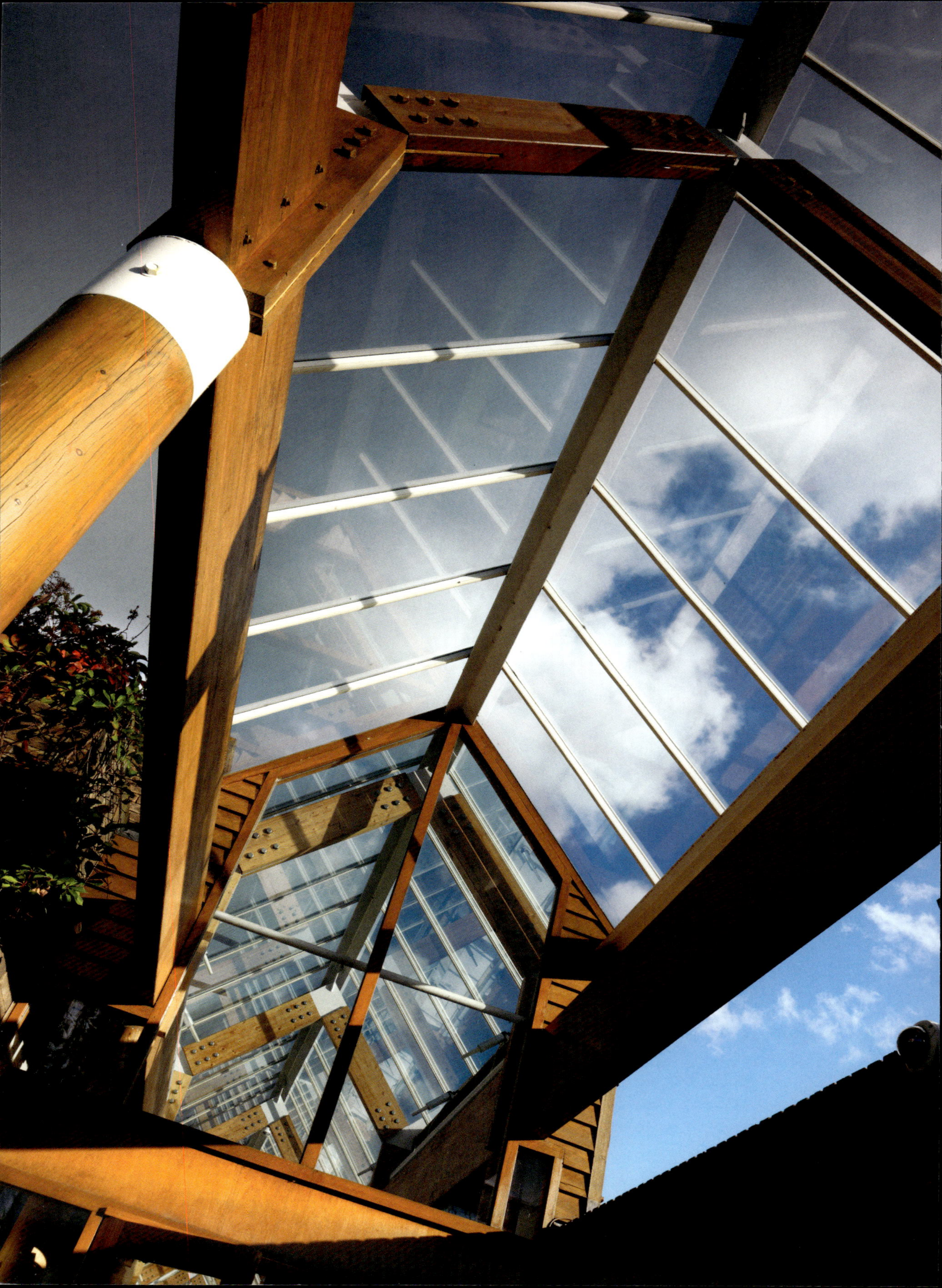

Hepworth Museum, St Ives, Cornwall; a third at Harvard University; exhibited, Tate Gallery, 1968. One of her most famous and distinctive works; the best-known and best-loved sculpture in the College, a regular backdrop for student photographs, and practically as iconic for the College as the Nemon sculpture of Winston on the Hall staircase. Everyone is free to walk through it. Since the 1990s it has become a place of communal remembrance at moments of tragedy; thus after 9/11. It replaced Hepworth's 'Squares with Two Circles' (1966), her original loan.

Barbara Hepworth (1903-75) lived at St Ives from 1939. Rejecting representation for abstraction, she described her aim 'to infuse the formal perfection of geometry with the vital grace of nature'. With Henry Moore, she defined British modernist sculpture in the 1950s. Her second husband was painter Ben Nicholson. In the 1960s befriended by Churchill's Vice-Master Kenneth McQuillen, who arranged the sculpture's coming; their correspondence is in the Archives Centre. See *Barbara Hepworth, A Pictorial Autobiography* (Tate Gallery, 1993).

South-east corner, by Staircase 37, a tulip tree (*Liriodendron Tulipifera*), given by Randolph Churchill, 1960. In front of the Archives Centre, a silver birch tree (*Betula Pendula*), given by Major-General Jack Hamilton, first Bursar, 1972. Western part of Great Court, by Staircase 55, a large ash tree (*Fraxinus Angustifolia*), given by Lady (Elizabeth) Cockcroft, 1966.

RESIDENTIAL COURTS. Described under 'Architecture' above. North Court (courts 1-3, Staircases 1-12, completed 1962) is detached from the others; East Court (courts 4-6, Staircases 31-42, completed 1964) is linked to South Court (courts 7-9, Staircases 43-52, completed 1967) by a covered walkway; West Court (court 10, Staircases 53-58, completed 1968) connects directly to South Court. In most colleges staircases are lettered; here they are numbered; mysteriously, Staircases 13-30 are forever non-existent. The naming of the courts has never been satisfactory (thus North Court is three courts, and so on), locations usually being denoted by staircase numbers; the naming of West Court as 'Wolfson Court' did not catch on. The 40 staircases each have on average 12 rooms or flats, making a total of 485, 60 of which are occupied by Fellows (as teaching rooms or residential 'sets'). In most courts the staircase principle is uncompromised; in South Court short corridors were introduced for economy. Originally, around 100 rooms were two-room student sets, a living room and separate bedroom, in traditional Oxbridge manner; the bedrooms were converted to provide ensuites, 1990s. Ground floor rooms were likewise extended to provide ensuites by tactful infilling into the open cloister. Each staircase has a bathroom, shower room, toilets, a 'bedder's' workroom, a trunk-room, and a kitchen for unambitious catering (on the assumption of dining in

RIGHT: 'Gemini' by Denis Mitchell

LEFT: The Study Centre provides seminar and training environments

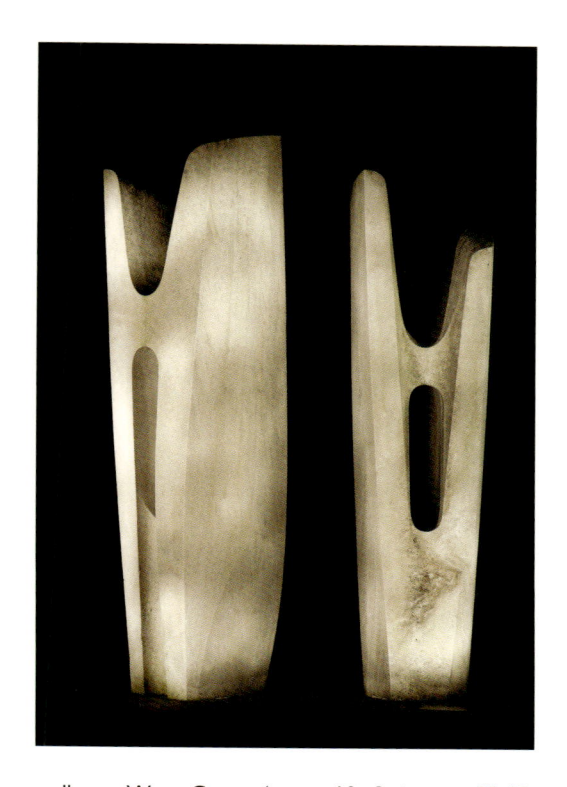

CHURCHILL COLLEGE CAMBRIDGE

51

Hall). Rooms are generally 15 sq. m. (160 sq. ft), 50 per cent larger than the national university norm for 1960. Each has its own washbasin and was centrally heated from the outset (modish luxuries in 1960). Two staircases, 1 and 35, are used by Fellows only. Room 48A remodelled, 1993, for disabled students. Window frames teak throughout. Original rubber stair and landing treads a gift of the Government of Malaya.

East Court: Winston's mulberry tree (see above); near Staircase 35, a bronze sculpture: 'Pointing Figure with Child' (1966) by **Bernard Meadows** (1915-2005), professor of sculpture at the Royal College of Art, purchased with the aid of the Arts Council. **North Court:** by Staircase 5, sculpture in cement and resin, 'Spiral' (1991), by **Michael Gillespie** (1929-), purchased 1993. **South Court**, by Staircase 48: a Maidenhair tree (*Gingko biloba*), 1970, a medicinal deciduous conifer.

FELLOWS' AND MASTER'S GARDENS.

The Fellows' Garden stands between North Court and the Buttery and Senior Common Room range. Centre tree: dawn redwood (*Metasequoia Glyptostroboides*), rare, originally from Kew Gardens, planted by Sir John and Lady Cockcroft, 1963. Sculpture, lead and aluminium, 'Crescent Moon Bull' (1998) by **Christine Fox** (1922-). Tree against SCR wall: magnolia (*Magnolia Grandiflora*), given by the SCR, 1966. North, beyond the trellis, the Master's Lodge and Garden.

PLAYING FIELDS.

Looking westwards from the Hepworth statue are the College's playing fields. To the left, six tennis courts (1991), replacing earlier courts on the Møller Centre site. Ahead, on the western boundary, the Chapel. Right: the Møller Centre with its distinctive octagonal tower. The tree line at the western perimeter divides the College from the University Observatory. Trees on the fields include: redbuds (*Cercis Canadensis*) given by Sir William Hawthorne (1977), a copper beech (*Fagus Sylvatica Purpurea*) given by Professor Andrew Phillipson (1977), and Norway maples (*Acer Platanoides 'Crimson King'*) given by Stephen Roskill (1977), these three west of South Court and east or south-east of tennis courts (Madingley Road bank); a Cambridge oak (*Quercus Warburgii*), rare, planted 2006, in memory of Alex Hopkins, south-west corner of tennis courts; a beech (*Fagus Sylvatica*) given by Richard ('Dick') Tizard (near south-west corner of North Court); Cappadocian maples (*Acer Cappadocicum*) given by Sir Alec Broers (1997), in the 'island' of the peripheral pathway; and a cedar (*Cedrus Deodara*) given by Sir Hermann and Lady Bondi (1990), south-east of the Chapel. Not on the fields, but along the Storey's Way frontage are notable trees: paper bark maple (*Acer Griseum*), 2001, left of pond; Persian ironwood (*Parrotica Persica*), 2003, corner of Madingley Road.

The College's western buildings, beyond the main body of the original College, may be approached either by the path along the periphery of the playing fields or via Churchill Road.

CHURCHILL ROAD.

Vehicular access is by private road running along the site's northern boundary, and is accessible at various points, such as Staircase 5. Named thus in 2004 (formerly drably 'The Private Road'). Increasingly the College's arterial spine, accessing the more recently constructed buildings. From the College entrance, in turn: staff car parks, Master's Lodge, North Court, Study Centre, Møller Centre, Wolfson Flats, Sheppard Flats, access to the Chapel. Also, garden access to College houses in Storey's Way. Front courtyard of the Master's Lodge: a Japanese garden, designed for Lady Boyd, 1997; opposite Lodge and Fellows' car park, two of the few surviving elms. In front of North Court, sculpture in mocca cream marble, 'Gemini' (1973), by **Denis Mitchell** (1912-93), given by Linden Holman in memory of James Holman CBE (1916-74).

STUDY CENTRE, MUSIC CENTRE, PAVILION.

A single-storey complex of buildings, standing between the main College and the Møller Centre. A palimpsest of four construction phases, progressively enlarged. The first, a sports Pavilion (1967), with gym, by **Richard Sheppard**, formerly venue for the weekly student disco now held in the Buttery, but still called 'the Pav'. Second, an extension (by **Sheppard**) to create Music Rooms (opened by Lady Mary Soames, 1980), comprising a recital room and four practice rooms; discontinued and reconfigured in 2007 to provide new offices and training rooms. Third, a Study Centre, designed by **Thurlow,**

The Music Centre and Study Centre Extension

Carnell, and Thornburrow, opened 1993, to provide seminar and social facilities for the Møller Centre. Thurlow drew the three buildings together by a long top-lit gallery. The Study Centre meeting rooms are fully glazed to the south, commanding views across the playing fields. Fourth, a new extension to the Study Centre, designed by **DSDHA** (Deborah Saunt and David Hills Architects) (construction by Haymills), 2007, (RIBA award 2009), in a starkly different style, abandoning brick and instead steel framed and clad in dark reflective glass; incorporating a new Music Centre. The combined study areas provide training spaces, ICT and business facilities, including 15 conference rooms offering a flexible and collaborative learning environment. Plaque in lounge: *Official Opening. Study Centre Development. Maersk McKinney Møller KBE. 16th November 2007*. The Study Centre (together with its parent, the Møller Centre) provides one of the finest displays of furniture designed by **Hans Wegner** (see below). Paintings: 'Marilyn Monroe' (1981) by **Andy Warhol** (1928-87) and **Pietro Psaier** (1936-2004); 'Sail' (1959) by **Hans Tisdall** (1910-97) (both on loan); 'Scroll' by **Margot Perryman** (1938-), purchased 2005.

The Music Centre comprises a recital room, practice room, and recording studio; opened by Lady Soames. The glass curtain wall of the Recital Room provides a visual link with the 'old' College and opens onto a terrace. College musicians and the choir perform here. Equipped with a Steinway Grand piano; and a double manual harpsichord, based on an instrument by Nicolas Blanchet (1733), designed and built (1983) by **David Rubio** of Cambridge (1934-2000). The whole complex is managed by the Møller Centre.

MØLLER CENTRE. Architect, **Henning Larsen** (1925-), opened 1992. Described in Part I under 'Architecture'. In the 'wedge' inset near the east end, south side, a foundation stone, carved by **David Kindersley's Workshop**: *Maersk McKinney Møller Building. This stone was laid on the 11th of June 1991 by the Lady Soames, DBE, to commemorate the generous benefaction of the Danish A. P. Møller Foundation*. In the entrance foyer a plaque: *Her Majesty Queen Ingrid of Denmark inaugurated this building, the Maersk McKinney Møller Centre for Continuing Education, on the 2nd of October 1992*. Entrance hall:

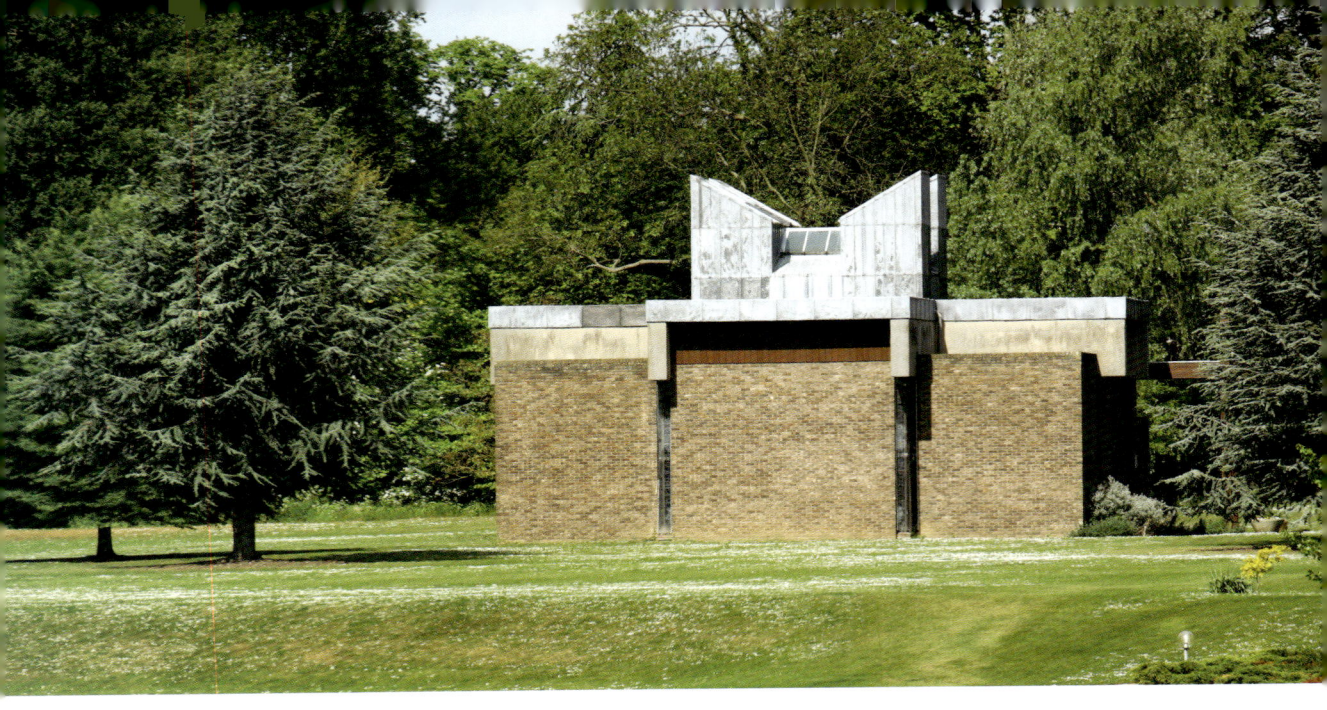

The Chapel

'Prospect (the Triptych)' by **Margot Perryman** (1938-), purchased 2003. At base of principal staircase: the 'Circle chair' (1986) by **Hans Wegner**.

> **Maersk McKinney Møller** (1913-) is Denmark's leading merchant shipping magnate and philanthropist. His father, Arnold Peter Møller (1876-1965), built the business; in the 1930s he sought to galvanise Denmark against the Nazis and was in touch with Winston Churchill; when Denmark capitulated in 1940 he ordered his ships into neutral ports; his son, Maersk, escaped to the USA to operate the 'free' navy, securing control for the Allies of all but two of the firm's 36 ships. Maersk became a partner, 1940; chair, 1965-2003, until aged 90; posts included chair of the Dansk Industri Syndikat, Odense Steel Shipyard, Danish Shipping Board. His charitable trust is named for his mother, Chastine Estelle McKinney, and father; his greatest benefaction is the Danish National Opera House. Honorary Fellow, 1991.

At the east end, three executive bedroom suites (formerly student kitchens and common rooms, then ICT room and gym): named the **Wegner, Larsen, and Svendborg Suites** (ground, first, and second floors, respectively).

> **Hans Wegner** (1915-2007), doyen of Danish furniture designers, who designed the furniture for the Centre; studied and taught at the Copenhagen School of Arts and Crafts; designer in Arne Jacobsen's architectural practice; then own practice from 1943. The 'Møller chair' (ash, steam-bent back, woven cord seat) was especially designed for the Centre in 1990. Note also the stunning 'Peacock chair' (1947).

> **Henning Larsen** (1925-), leading Danish architect; internationally known for the Ministry of Foreign Affairs building in Riyadh and the Copenhagen Opera House.

> **Svendborg**: Danish town where the Maersk Company was founded in 1904 by Capt. Peter Maersk Møller, grandfather of Maersk McKinney Møller; and the name of the Company's first container ship, launched 1973.

SHEPPARD FLATS. The Sheppard Flats provide 20 flats for visiting scholars, the first part of the College built (1960-1); named after the architect. Two storeys, an intriguing labyrinth of courtyards and alleyways, almost in the style of a Mediterranean hill village, much admired by architects for its intricate planning and intimate spaces. Each flat has a secluded walled patio and large sliding windows. The overall ground plan is swastika-shaped: an ironic joke for Winston Churchill's college. The College began here, flats serving as offices, teaching rooms, and library, until 1964. Refurbished, 2002-6.

Sir Richard Sheppard (1910-82), CBE, RA, FRIBA, founder of Sheppard Robson Architects; educated, Architectural Association School; author of *Building for the People* (1945); designed numerous schools, 1950s; and universities, 1960s-70s, including Brunel, City, Loughborough, and Manchester Metropolitan; his winning of the Churchill competition a breakthrough for modernism in British university architecture.

West of the Flats, the Groundsman's Compound (1993), replacing the original, by the Pavilion, demolished to make way for the Study Centre.

THE CHAPEL stands near the western periphery, 500 metres from the Porters' Lodge. Opened, 15 October 1967, by Lady Cockcroft, five weeks after the sudden death of her husband, the first Master. Designed on the Byzantine model, with a central rather than east-west plan, abandoning the traditional nave and chancel, in keeping with the liturgical innovations of the 1960s. 14.6 sq. m. (48 sq. ft.). Majestic concrete piers and beams, brick walls, slit windows. Cool, austere, dark, enclosing. The external appearance chunky and muscular, but graceful within, the concrete beams emphatically marking the Greek cross. Timber roof; skylight over the crossing, with diagonally cut-off tops, copper clad. Seats 100. Over the entrance, a 150 lb bell from the aircraft carrier HMS Hermes, launched by Lady Spencer-Churchill; acquired by Stephen Roskill. Plaque: *This bell was presented to the Churchill College Chapel by the Admiralty Board, 1967, in memory of Sir Winston Churchill, First Lord of the Admiralty, 1911-15 and 1939-40.* There are eight windows, 'The Elements' (1970), designed by **John Piper**, fabricated by **Patrick Reyntiens** (1925-). The theme is 'Let there be light' (Genesis 1:3). East: humanity's search for truth and God's revelation. West: humanity's industry and God's creativity. North: humanity's search for beauty and God's response. South: humanity's search for love and God's response. In blue, mauve, gold, and green.

John Piper (1903-92), Britain's foremost 20th-century artist in stained glass. Work may be seen at Robinson College (Cambridge), Nuffield College (Oxford), Coventry Cathedral, Liverpool Catholic Cathedral, Eton College, Oundle School, SS Peter and Paul Church, Aldeburgh (Benjamin Britten memorial window), and St Peter's Church, Babraham, Cambridgeshire.

Inside, two plaques on the north wall, Welsh slate, respectively by **William Carter** and **David Parsley**. First plaque: *The windows in this chapel were given in memory of Sir John Cockcroft OM, first Master of Churchill College, by Lady Cockcroft, his family and friends throughout the world. Designed and made by John Piper and Patrick Reyntiens.* Second plaque: *In grateful memory of John Noel Duckworth MA TD, Canon of Accra, 23 December 1912 – 24 November 1980, first chaplain of Churchill College 1961-73.* By the vestry door, a cartoon of Duckworth in a Japanese POW camp, by **Ronald Searle** (b.1920), including extracts from Russell Braddon's *The Naked Island* (1951), dedicated to Duckworth, 'who lived more fearlessly and more gently than all others'.

Canon Noel Duckworth (1912-80), first College chaplain, 1961-73, much beloved among early students; educated, St John's College; cox of the Cambridge boat crew, 1934-6, and of British crew at Hitler's Berlin Olympics, 1936; captured by the Japanese at the fall of Singapore, 1942, and survived POW camps; saved many lives by his camaraderie and skilful defiance in dealing with their captors; featured in the popular 1950s television show *This is Your Life*. Chaplain, St John's College, 1946-8; Senior Tutor, University College, Gold Coast (Ghana), 1948-58.

The altar originally placed centrally, with three-dimensional hanging cross (wood, metal, silver-gilt), designed by **Keith Thyssen** of Sheffield (c.1966); this and four wooden candlesticks with gilt bowls given by the Goldsmiths' Company. Stone font designed by **Peter Sellwood**, given by St Peter's School, Huntingdon. Altar table given by Revd Dr A. C. Bouquet. Lecterns designed by the architect; given by the contractor. Organ by **E. J. Johnson** of Cambridge (1973), two manuals with pedals and electric action. Yamaha grand piano, purchased by the College (1982) with a grant from the Coral Samuel Charitable Trust. 'Coventry chairs' designed by renowned furniture designer **Gordon Russell** (1892-1980).

The Chapel's surprising location at the extremity of the College site is owing to a controversy at the time of the founding. Some Fellows urged that a modern scientific college had no business building a place of worship to a God who isn't; Francis Crick, decoder of DNA, resigned his Fellowship in protest. Others were equally vehement in favour. A compromise was reached: the Chapel was built on land leased to a Chapel Trust, consisting of Fellows who wanted a chapel. The Chapel Trust appoints a chaplain, but the College employs a (secular) counsellor. The Chapel's cost was borne by **Timothy Beaumont**. Plaque in baptistery: *In thanksgiving for the life of Revd Timothy Wentworth Beaumont, The Lord Beaumont of Whitley, 22 November 1928 – 8 April 2008, whose benefaction made the building of this chapel possible.*

> **Timothy Beaumont** (1928-2008), priest, politician, author, philanthropist. Educated at Oxford; after a career in publishing, 1960s (chair, Studio Vista Books; proprietor, *New Christian*), turned to politics, becoming chair and president of the Liberal Party, 1967-70; Liberal peer, 1967; later, front bench spokesman in the House of Lords for the Liberal Democrats; latterly the sole Green Party member of the Lords. In 1961, the future bishop, Hugh Montefiore, persuaded him to donate £30,000 for the Churchill Chapel.

The dell behind the Chapel was a rubbish tip for St John's College in Victorian times and domestic artefacts sometimes appear. Thousands of daffodils bloom in spring.

A CAMBRIDGE VISTA. The western end of the College site lies at the start of Madingley Rise and is 9 m. (30 ft) above the eastern end. Standing at the Chapel's east side, a Cambridge city roofscape is visible, one mile away. Prominent buildings, left to right: spire of All Saints' Church, Jesus Lane (right of Dining Hall); square tower of St John's College Chapel (straight ahead); tower of Great St Mary's Church (the University Church); the Engineering Lab in Corn Exchange Street; the pinnacled roof of King's College Chapel (and behind it the spire of the Catholic Church). Round to the right, tower of the University Library. Far right, on Madingley Road, parallel with the Chapel, laboratories of West Cambridge.

WOLFSON FLATS. North side of Churchill Road, the Wolfson Flats (1967), the only early part of the College not designed by Sheppard; instead by **David Roberts** (1911-82), prolific local architect. 40 flats for postgraduate students with partners or families; three storeys, the first two providing maisonettes. In contrast with Sheppard's buildings, brick without concrete frame, and Cambridge yellow brick instead of Lincolnshire brown. Three sides of a courtyard, but more like a three-sided terraced street, each flat having its entrance on the outer side. The external walkway for the upper storey is corbelled. Major refurbishment and remodelling, 2009-10, including extensions on the courtyard side, new fenestration and cladding.

BROERS, BONDI, AND HAWTHORNE HOUSES (respectively, 40A-C Storey's Way). Built 2001-2, opened 2003, providing 30 rooms for postgraduate students, 10 in each. After a limited competition, architects **Cottrell and Vermeulen** were chosen (practice associate Simon Tucker a Churchill alumnus); construction by C. G. Franklin. Nicknamed 'beehives' or 'pepperpots'. Arresting shapes: two flat planes, two sloping. Precast concrete cladding echoes the College buildings, while low-slung tiled walls (handmade Sussex clay tiles) reflect adjacent Arts and Crafts houses. Tiles in the entrance canopy soffits show images of the atomic structure of silicon. The design aims to be domestic and non-institutional, the houses emphasising community, each having a large

RIGHT: John Piper's stained glass in the chapel

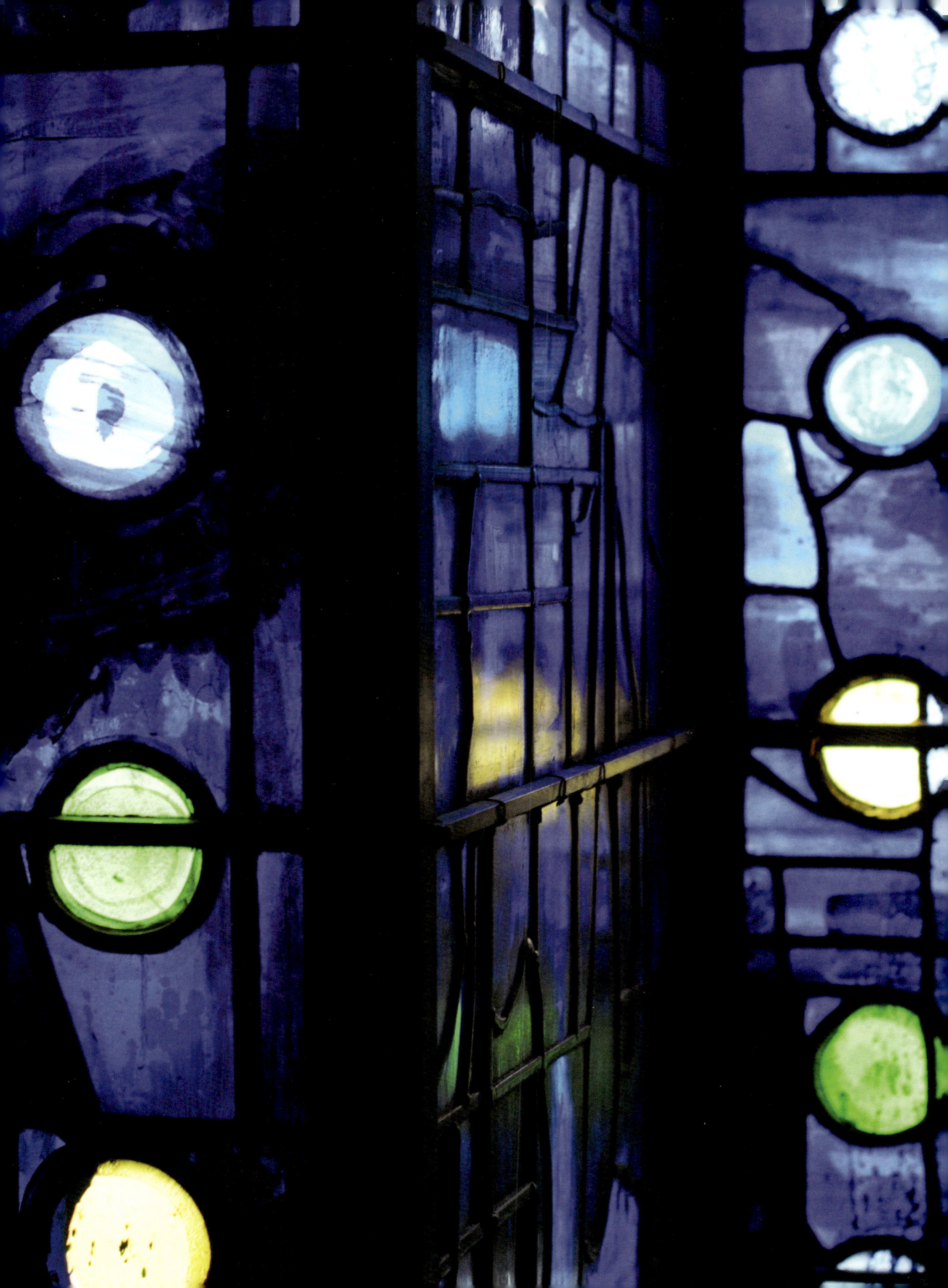

One of three postgraduate houses, opened in 2003

common room, large kitchen, and generous circulation space. (The common room is on a different floor in each house.) Each has a large staircase window, with a bench to look out at the trees; light streams out at night. All rooms are at corners, giving a double aspect; quirkily angular, their ceilings and walls not quite perpendicular; each has an ensuite unit, fridge, and 10 sockets for the IT age. 40A has two rooms for disabled students and 40B has seminar rooms. The orchard of two dozen cherry trees (*Prunus Taihaku*) is integral to the scheme. Costing £2 million, the first College building to benefit significantly from alumni donations. Winner of the David Urwin award for the best new building in Cambridgeshire, 1998-2002. Named in 2006 after the second, third, and fourth Masters.

Sir William Hawthorne (1913-), CBE, FRS, FREng; aeronautical engineer; Master, 1967-83; educated, Westminster School, Trinity College, Cambridge; assisted Sir Frank Whittle in jet engine development, 1940s; professor, MIT, 1941-51; Professor of Applied Thermodynamics, Cambridge, 1951-80; head, Engineering Department, 1968-73; foreign associate, US National Academy of Sciences.

Sir Hermann Bondi (1919-2005), KCB, FRS; mathematician and cosmologist; Master, 1983-90; born, Vienna, emigrated under shadow of Nazism; educated Trinity College, Cambridge; radar research in wartime; lecturer, Cambridge, 1945-54; Professor of Mathematics, King's College, London, 1954-71; head, European Space Research Organisation, 1967-

71; chief scientific adviser, Ministry of Defence, 1971-7; president, British Humanist Association, 1982-99. Autobiography: *Science, Churchill, and Me* (1990).

Sir Alec Broers (1938-), Lord Broers (2004), FRS, FREng; electron microscopist and nanotechnologist; Master, 1990-6; educated, Melbourne, Cambridge; IBM research staff, USA, 1965-84; Professor of Electrical Engineering, Cambridge, 1984-96; Vice-Chancellor, Cambridge, 1996-2003; president, Royal Academy of Engineering, 2001-6; chair, House of Lords Committee on Science and Technology, 2004-7; Reith Lecturer, 2005; foreign associate, US National Academy of Engineering. See Broers, *The Triumph of Technology* (2005).

A pathway from these houses leads to Storey's Way.

STOREY'S WAY. The street, built 1911, is named after a 17th-century Cambridge bookseller and philanthropist; a designated Conservation Area. Seven houses are Listed Buildings, fine Arts and Crafts and neo-Georgian residences (Nos. 29, 30, 48, 54, 56, 63, 76). Besides 40A-C, the College owns six houses: Nos. 36, 44, 64, 70, 72, 76. No. 36 is leased to the property management firm Davis Langdon; others are used for student and Fellows' accommodation; Cambridge University Radio broadcasts from No. 72.

No. 44, Whittinghame Lodge, the first house purchased by the College (the Wolfson Flats were built in its garden), was the first home of the University's Department of Genetics. Plaque in the porch: *Given to the University in 1914 by the Rt Hon. A. J. Balfour MP and the Rt Hon. the Lord Esher GCB GCVO, for the use of the Arthur Balfour Professor of Genetics: R. C. Punnett 1912, R. A. Fisher 1943, J. M. Thoday 1959. Sold to Churchill College 1962. This plaque was erected by the College to mark the centenary of Sir Ronald Fisher FRS, 17th February 1990.*

Arthur Balfour, OM, FRS (1848-1930), Prime Minister, 1902-5, President of the British Academy, 1921-8 (and turned down invitation to be simultaneously President of the Royal Society),

Sir William Hawthorne, second Master, aeronautical engineer

Sir Hermann Bondi, third Master, mathematician and cosmologist

CHURCHILL COLLEGE CAMBRIDGE

Chancellor of the University, brother-in-law of scientist **Lord Rayleigh** and philosopher **Henry Sidgwick**. Whittinghame House, East Lothian, Scotland, his family home. **Sir Ronald Fisher** (1890-1962), Fellow of Gonville and Caius College, statistician and geneticist; his and J. B. S. Haldane's work marked a turning point in the acceptance of Darwin's theory of natural selection; an enthusiast for eugenics. See J. Box, *R. A Fisher* (1978).

From 1990 to 2000 the College owned No. 48, the finest house in the street: 1913, by **Hugh Baillie-Scott** (1865-1945) (who also designed Nos. 29, 30, 54, and 56, 1914-22). Influenced by, though less well-known than, Edwin Lutyens and Charles Voysey, Baillie-Scott belonged to the Arts and Crafts Movement, striving to recreate an English vernacular, in this case a Tudor manor house. The interior, spartan but beautiful in its feel for natural materials, is reminiscent of Charles Rennie Mackintosh's work. The house was extensively renovated by the College. See J. D. Kornwolf, *Baillie Scott* (1972); D. Haigh in *Architect's Journal* (22 July 1992).

No. 76, Storey's End (by the entrance to Churchill Road), was designed (1913) by **A. H. Moberly**, for the University's first Professor of Economic History, Sir John Clapham (1873-1946). At his retirement in 1938 it was bought by Dr Edward Bevan, a general practitioner, who, with his wife Joan, took paying guests, generally posh girls in search of well-born undergraduate husbands. There were two distinguished paying guests: **Ludwig Wittgenstein**, one of the 20th century's most important philosophers, who died here; and **Princess Margrethe of Denmark** (now queen), while she was an undergraduate reading Archaeology and Anthropology at Girton College. Purchased by the College, 1991. The garden cedarwood surgery and waiting room were converted, 1994, for use as a drama and creative arts studio. Plaque: *Ludwig Wittgenstein, 1889-1951, Philosopher, Engineer, Architect, Artist, lived here*. 'Do not agree with me in particular opinions but investigate the matter in the right way. To notice the interesting things ... that serve as keys if you use them properly'.

ENVIRONS. These notes are confined to locations worth a visit within 500 metres of the College perimeter. South of the Storey's Way junction with Madingley Road (footpath access) lies the Centre for Mathematical Sciences in a stunning ensemble of buildings, by Edward Cullinan (1999-2001). South-west, along Madingley Road, toward the M11 motorway, lies Cambridge West, a major site for University development for the sciences, graduate and postdoctoral accommodation, and the university-business interface. Buildings include the Cavendish Lab (1974), Whittle Lab (1973), William Gates Computing Lab (2001), Centres for Nanoscience (2003) and Physics of Medicine (2008), Schofield Centre (2001), Broers Building (2010), and Veterinary School (1955). New roads are named after great Cambridge scientists: James Clerk Maxwell, J. J. Thompson, Charles Babbage. The Schofield Centre is named after Churchill Fellow **Andrew Schofield**, pioneer in soil mechanics, and the Broers Building after the fourth Master, **Lord Broers**.

Back toward the City, four other colleges occupy the wedge formed by Madingley and Huntingdon Roads: immediately adjacent in Storey's Way are Fitzwilliam College (Gatehouse Court, 2002-4) and Murray Edwards College (formerly New Hall), (together with Trinity Hall's Wychfield site, 2004-7). These were built on properties owned by **Charles Darwin's** widow, Emma, and two sons, Horace and Francis Darwin: The Grove (1813), The Orchard (1882), Wychfield House (1884). St Edmund's and Lucy Cavendish Colleges are a short way east. Such is Cambridge's topography that these are collectively called the 'Colleges on the Hill'. Opposite No. 68 Storey's Way is a Trinity Hall stone waymark, by the Cardozo Kindersley Workshop (2006), with that College's crescent symbol and a manicule pointing to the College's city-centre home,

RIGHT: The Møller Centre: at the sharp end

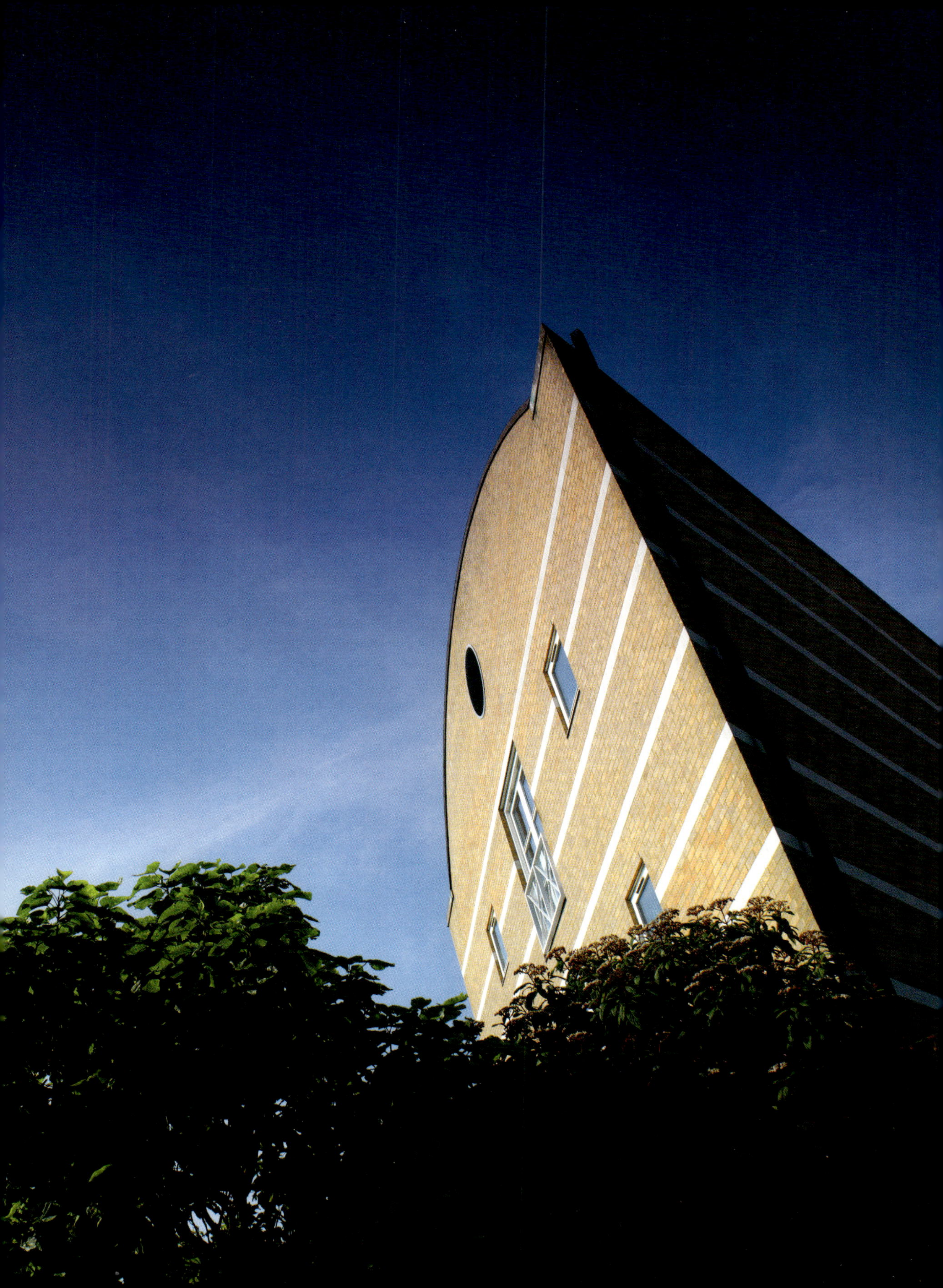

The squash court wall in autumn

2006 metres away. North-west of the College is the University Farm, due for development by the University for residential housing and research facilities. The site opposite the College's frontage was developed for housing by St John's College in 1992. There is another college 'colony' close at hand, Girton College's Wolfson Court, Clarkson Road. Just off Clarkson Road is Cockcroft Place, the only Cambridge street named after a member of Churchill.

Adjacent to the College's western boundary (accessible at several points) is the Institute of Astronomy campus. The earliest building is the **University Observatory**; Greek Doric style (J. C. Mead, 1823). It lies on an exact east-west axis, with a sightline due south to Grantchester Church spire to mark the meridian. It replaced **Isaac Newton's** observatory on the Great Gate of Trinity College. The Northumberland Telescope (1838), for many years one of the world's largest refracting telescopes, is still used by the University Astronomical Society and open to the public for observing; the 36-inch telescope (1951-5) is the largest optical telescope in Britain. In 1841 the future University Observer John Couch Adams predicted the existence of Neptune, but the discovery was made by the German J. G. Galle in 1846. North of the Observatory is Greenwich House (1989), briefly home to the Royal Greenwich Observatory (1990-8). Beyond, the Hoyle Building (1968) commemorates astronomer Sir Fred Hoyle (statue on the lawn by Sheila Solomon, 1992), who worked closely with Churchill's third master **Sir Hermann Bondi** on the Steady State theory of the universe. The latest addition is the Kavli Institute of Cosmology (2009). Next westward is the Earth Sciences Department: the Bullard Laboratories are named after the Churchill College geophysicist **Sir Edward Bullard** (1907-80). A foot and cycle path, Adam's Walk, runs from the College around the Astronomy campus and offers a traffic-free route to West Cambridge and beyond to the village of Coton.

A stone's throw from the College's north-west boundary, but accessed from Huntingdon Road, down All Souls Lane (between Nos. 145 and 147), is the fascinating **Ascension Burial Ground**, opened 1869, remarkable for its assemblage of deceased academic distinction. There are two Nobel Prizewinners (**Cockcroft**, the first Master, splitter of the atom, and Sir Frederick Gowland Hopkins, discoverer of vitamins); seven members of the Order of Merit (the literary critic Sir Richard Jebb, the philosopher G. E. Moore, the astrophysicist Sir Arthur Eddington, the anthropologist J. G. Frazer, the classicist Henry Jackson, together with Cockcroft and Hopkins); 15 knights; eight Masters of Colleges; and 50 people with entries in the *Oxford Dictionary of National Biography*. Here lie the philosopher **Ludwig Wittgenstein** (much the most visited grave); economist Alfred Marshall (who gives his name to the Economics Faculty library); composer Charles Wood; poet Frances Cornford (friend of Rupert Brooke) who lies with her husband Francis Cornford, classicist and author of the famous squib on University politics, *Microcosmographica Cantabridgiensis* (1908); historian Sir Denis Brogan; criminologist Sir Leon Radzinowicz; mathematician and philosopher Frank Ramsey, dead at 26; astronomer John Couch Adams; architect David Roberts, who designed more of the University's 20th-century buildings than any other architect; the brave young Bridget Spufford, who names the University's trust for disabled students; two sons of Charles Darwin, Sir Francis and Sir Horace, respectively botanist and scientific instrument maker; pioneer female student Charlotte Scott who stunned the University by coming unofficial eighth in the Mathematics Tripos in 1880, forcing it to allow women to sit the exams officially. The former chapel (1875) is now the studio and 'alphabet museum' of stone-cutter Eric Marland. The cemetery encapsulates a century-and-a-half of the University's modern history.

A number of nearby streets have fine early examples of modernist domestic architecture. Notable are 31 Madingley Road (Marshall Sisson, 1931-2); 9 Wilberforce Road (Dora Cosens, 1937); and Willow House (formerly Thurso), Conduit Head Road (George Checkley, 1932-3). At No. 12 Bulstrode Gardens a plaque marks the home of the literary critics F. R. Leavis and Q. D. Leavis, who lived there, 1962-81, and loathed Churchill College as a monster of philistine utilitarianism. No. 173 Huntingdon Road is Kapitza House, designed by H. C. Hughes (c.1930) for **Piotr Kapitza** (1894-1984), FRS, Soviet Nobel physicist, friend and collaborator of Cockcroft in the Cavendish Lab in the 1930s, Honorary Fellow of Churchill College. The house was managed by the College on behalf of the Soviet Academy of Sciences, 1966-90, and Cold War era alumni recollect lodging uneasily alongside Soviet visiting scientists. It is a strange paradox that Churchill College should include among its Honorary Fellows Winston Churchill, who galvanised the West in his 'Iron Curtain' speech of 1946, and Piotr Kapitza, Order of Lenin, Hero of Soviet Labour, one of the begetters of the Soviet atomic bomb. In 1965, Cockcroft and Kapitza, after decades of separation, were reunited at Churchill College, and held a final meeting of the Kapitza Club, in abeyance since its Cavendish Lab heyday in the 1930s.

ELIZABETH THE SECOND

by the Grace of God of the United Kingdom of Great Britain and Northern Ireland and of Our other Realms and Territories Queen, Head of the Commonwealth, Defender of the Faith.

TO ALL TO WHOM THESE PRESENTS SHALL COME, GREETING!

WHEREAS a Petition has been presented unto Us by Our right trusty and well-beloved Counsellor Sir Winston Leonard Spencer Churchill, Knight of Our Most Noble Order of the Garter, Member of the Order of Merit, Member of the Order of the Companions of Honour; Our right trusty and well-beloved Edgar Douglas Baron Adrian, Member of the Order of Merit; Our trusty and well-beloved Noel Gilroy Annan, Officer of Our Most Excellent Order of the British Empire, and William John Carron, Esquires; Our right trusty and well-beloved Counsellor Oliver Viscount Chandos, Companion of Our Distinguished Service Order, upon whom has been conferred the Decoration of the Military Cross; Our trusty and well-beloved Sir John Douglas Cockcroft, Member of the Order of Merit, Knight Commander of Our Most Honourable Order of the Bath, Commander of Our Most Excellent Order of the British Empire; Brian Westerdale Downs, Esquire; Sir Alexander Fleck, Knight Commander of Our Most Excellent Order of the British Empire; Our right trusty and well-beloved Frederick Baron Godber; Marshal of Our Royal Air Force Our right trusty and well-beloved Arthur William Baron Tedder, Knight Grand Cross of Our Most Honourable Order of the Bath; Our trusty and well-beloved Sir Alexander Robertus Todd, Knight and Our right trusty and well-beloved Ronald Morce Baron Weeks, Knight Commander of Our Most Honourable Order of the Bath, Commander of Our Most Excellent Order of the British Empire, Companion of Our Distinguished Service Order, upon whom have been conferred the Decoration of the Military Cross and the Territorial Decoration, which sheweth:

That funds have been raised by public subscription to establish and carry on at Cambridge a College to be called Churchill College as a memorial to the said Sir Winston Leonard Spencer Churchill:

That the Petitioners are the trustees of those funds and hold the same upon the trusts of a trust deed dated the sixth day of May in the year of our Lord One thousand nine hundred and fifty-eight (the trustees for the time being of which trust deed are hereinafter called "the Churchill Trustees"):

And that the Petitioners as such trustees have begun the building of the College and have appointed a Master-elect thereof, namely the said Sir John Douglas Cockcroft and have appointed certain Fellows-designate thereof and that the said College will shortly open for the reception of students:

AND WHEREAS by the said Petition the Petitioners have most humbly prayed that We would be graciously pleased to grant a Charter in such terms as might seem to Us proper for the purpose of constituting the Master, Fellows and Scholars of the said College a body corporate:

AND WHEREAS We have taken the said Petition into Our Royal Consideration and are minded to accede thereto.

NOW THEREFORE KNOW YE that We by virtue of Our Royal Prerogative in that behalf and of all other powers enabling Us so to do of Our especial grace, certain knowledge and mere motion have granted, willed, directed and ordained and by these Presents do for Us, Our Heirs and Successors grant, will, direct and ordain as follows:

APPENDICES

Appendix 1: Chronology

1949	Winston Churchill's speech at Massachusetts Institute of Technology
1950	Shell Petroleum puts the case for an institute of advanced technology
1955	Winston's conversation in Sicily about the need for a technology college
1957	John Colville and Alexander Todd seek to place the project in Cambridge
1958	University authorises the College; Trustees created; Appeal launched
1959	Site acquired; Winston plants a tree; Richard Sheppard chosen architect
1959	Sir John Cockcroft chosen Master; first meeting of Governing Body
1960	Royal Charter granted; the College opens, admitting its first postgraduates
1961	First building, Sheppard Flats, completed
1961	First undergraduates admitted; controversy over a chapel
1964	Central buildings, including Dining Hall, opened; first May Ball
1965	Library and Wolfson Hall opened
1965	Soviet physicist Piotr Kapitza reunited with Sir John Cockcroft at Churchill
1966	Full Collegiate status in the University; Trustees stood down
1966	Anti-Vietnam War demonstration against American ambassador
1967	A chapel at Churchill opened; Wolfson Flats opened
1968	Completion of the courtyards
1969	First men's college to decide to admit women; final May Ball
1969	Student representatives admitted to College Council
1969	Winston Churchill's post-1945 papers gifted to the College
1970	Undergraduate secures national student right to vote in university constituencies
1970	Student team wins TV's national *University Challenge* competition
1971	First woman Fellow elected
1972	First women students admitted
1973	Churchill Archives Centre opened
1974	Radio astronomer Antony Hewish awarded Nobel Prize
1978	Women's boat Head of the River (and on five further occasions to 1990)
1979	Physiologist Robert Edwards creates world's first IVF ('test tube') baby
1979	Cambridge University Radio starts broadcasting from a Churchill basement
1980	Music Rooms opened
1985	The first Roskill Memorial Lecture
1992	Opening of the Møller Centre for Continuing Education
1993	College achieves Listed Building status; Study Centre opened
1995	Winston Churchill's archive purchased by the National Lottery Heritage Fund
1996	Fourth Master, Alec Broers, appointed University Vice-Chancellor

1997	Archives Centre acquires Prime Minister Margaret Thatcher's papers
2000	Non-academic staff representatives admitted to College Council
2002	Archives Centre Extension opened
2002	Hawthorne, Bondi, and Broers Houses (for postgraduates) opened
2005	Student representatives admitted to Governing Body
2007	Study Centre Extension and Music Centre opened
2007	First alumnus to be elected to an Honorary Fellowship (Njabulo Ndebele)
2008	First alumnus to win a Nobel Prize (Roger Tsien)
2009	Lady Soames plants a tree 50 years after her father

Appendix 2: Masters

1959	Sir John Cockcroft, OM, CBE, FRS (1897-1967), Nobel physicist, who split the atom
1968	Sir William Hawthorne, CBE, FRS, FREng (1913-), aeronautical engineer, who helped develop the jet engine
1983	Sir Hermann Bondi, CBE, FRS (1919-2005), mathematician and cosmologist, who helped develop the Steady State theory of the universe
1990	Sir Alec Broers, FRS, FREng (1938-) (later Lord Broers), nanotechnologist, who became University Vice-Chancellor
1997	Sir John Boyd, KCMG, (1936-), diplomat, former ambassador to Japan
2006	Sir David Wallace, CBE, FRS, FREng (1945-), theoretical physicist, former Vice-Chancellor of Loughborough University

Appendix 3: Founder Trustees

Edgar Adrian, Baron Adrian, OM, FRS (1889-1977), Nobel physiologist
Noel Annan, Baron Annan (1916-2000), historian and educationist
William Carron, Baron Carron (1902-69), president, Amalgamated Engineering Union
Sir Winston Churchill, KG, PC, OM (1874-1965), Prime Minister, the Founder
Sir John Cockcroft, OM, FRS (1897-1967), Nobel physicist, first Master
Sir John Colville (1915-87), wartime private secretary to Winston Churchill
Brian Downs (1893-1984), linguist, University Vice-Chancellor
Alexander Fleck, Baron Fleck, FRS (1889-1968), Chair, Imperial Chemical Industries
Frederick Godber, Baron Godber (1888-1976), Chair, Shell Petroleum
Edward Knollys, Viscount Knollys (1895-1966), Chair, Vickers Aircraft
Oliver Lyttleton, Viscount Chandos, PC, MC (1893-1972), statesman, businessman
Arthur Tedder, Baron Tedder (1890-1967), Marshall of the Royal Air Force
Alexander Todd, Baron Todd, OM, FRS (1907-97), Nobel chemist
Ronald Weeks, Baron Weeks, CBE, MC (1890-1960), former Chair, Vickers Aircraft

Appendix 4: Honorary Fellows

1964	Sir Winston Churchill, KG, PC, OM (1874-1965), Prime Minister, the Founder
1965	Francis Crick, OM, FRS (1916-2004), Nobel molecular biologist
1965	John Morrison (1913-2000), classicist, first Vice-Master and Senior Tutor
1965	Sir Isaac Wolfson, FRS (1897-1991), businessman and philanthropist
1965	Randolph Churchill (1911-68), politician, author, journalist, Founder's son
1965	Henry Moore, OM, FBA (1898-1986), sculptor
1965	Sir Barnes Wallis, CBE, FRS (1887-1979), aircraft engineer and inventor

1968	Winston Churchill (1940-), politician, author, journalist, Founder's grandson
1971	Lord (Alexander) Todd, OM, FRS (1907-97), Nobel chemist
1971	Sir John Colville (1915-87), wartime private secretary to Winston Churchill
1976	Piotr Kapitza, FRS, Order of Lenin (1894-1984), Soviet Nobel physicist
1983	Lady Mary Soames, LG, DBE (1922-), author, Founder's daughter
1985	Lord (Richard) Adrian, FRS (1927-95), physiologist, Master of Pembroke College
1988	Lord (Noel) Annan (1916-2000), historian and educationist
1988	Garfield (Garry) Weston (1927-2002), businessman and philanthropist
1989	Ernest Walton (1903-95), Nobel physicist, split the atom with Cockcroft
1991	Maersk Mc-Kinney Møller, KBE (1913-), Danish shipowner and philanthropist
1995	Lord (Michael) Young, FBA (1915-2002), socialist, sociologist, educationist
2000	Sir Colin St John (Sandy) Wilson, RA (1922-2007), architect
2007	Sir John Gurdon, FRS (1933-), cell biologist, Master of Magdalene College
2007	Njabulo Ndebele (1948-), South African novelist and Vice-Chancellor, Cape Town, alumnus
2008	Sir Martin Gilbert, CBE (1936-), historian, biographer of Winston Churchill
2009	Roger Tsien (1952-), Nobel chemist, alumnus

Appendix 5: Distinguished Fellows

F = Fellow (dates of Fellowship in brackets)

Nobel Laureates: Fellows
Sir John Cockcroft (1897-1967; Master 1959-67) *Physics, 1951*
    'the transmutation of atomic nuclei by artificially accelerated atomic particles'
Francis Crick (1916-2004; F 1960-2) *Physiology/Medicine, 1962*
    'co-discovering the structure of DNA'
Antony Hewish (1924-; F 1961-) *Physics, 1974*
    'development of radio aperture synthesis and its role in the discovery of pulsars'

Nobel Laureates: Overseas Fellows
Philip Anderson (F 1961-2) *Physics, 1977*
    'electronic structure of magnetic and disordered systems'

Honorary Fellows: left to right: Sir John Gurdon, cell biologist; Lady Mary Soames, the Founder's daughter; Maersk McKinney Møller, shipowner and philanthropist; Njabulo Nbedele, novelist and alumnus

Sir David Wallace, sixth Master, theoretical physicist

Kenneth Arrow (F 1963-64, 1970, 1973, 1986) *Economics, 1972*
    'contributions to general economic equilibrium theory and welfare theory'
Felix Bloch (F 1967) *Physics, 1952*
    'new methods for nuclear magnetic precision measurements'
Gerard Debreu (F 1972) *Economics, 1983*
    'new analytical methods in economic theory and reformulation of the theory of general equilibrium'
Murray Gell-Mann (F 1966) *Physics, 1969*
    'work on the theory of elementary particles'
Vitali Ginsburg (F 1967) *Physics, 2003*
    'pioneering contributions to the theory of superconductors and superfluids'
Roald Hoffman (F 1978) *Chemistry, 1981*
    'theory concerning the course of chemical reactions'
Har Gobind Khorana (F 1967) *Physiology/Medicine, 1968*
    'interpretation of the genetic code and its function in protein synthesis'
Arthur Kornberg (F 1970) *Physiology/Medicine, 1959*
    'discovery of mechanisms in the biological synthesis of DNA'
William Lipscomb (F 1966) *Chemistry, 1976*
    'studies on the structure of boranes illuminating problems of chemical bonding'
Eric Maskin (F 1980-2) *Economics, 2007*
    'laying the foundations of mechanism design theory'

Octavio Paz (F 1970) *Literature, 1990*
    'impassioned writing with wide horizons characterised by sensuous intelligence and humanistic integrity'
Robert Solow (F 1983-4) *Economics, 1987*
    'contributions to the theory of economic growth'
Wole Soyinka (F 1973-4) *Literature, 1986*
    'in a wide cultural perspective and with poetic overtones he fashions the drama of existence'
George Wald (F 1963-4) *Physiology/Medicine, 1967*
    'discoveries concerning the primary physiological and chemical visual processes in the eye'
James Watson (F 1962) *Physiology/Medicine, 1962*
    'co-discovering the structure of DNA'

In addition, five Nobel Laureates among Honorary Fellows, including one alumnus (Churchill, Kapitza, Todd, Tsien, Walton).

Some leading scientists and technologists (excluding Overseas Fellows)
Includes all Fellows of the Royal Society, Fellows of the Royal Academy of Engineering, and members of the US National Academy of Sciences.

Lord (Richard) Adrian, FRS (1927-95; F 1960-81) *Physiology*
Gehan Amaratunga, FREng (1956-; F 1987-95, 1998-) *Engineering*
Michael Ashburner, FRS (1942-; F 1980-) *Genetics*
Alan Baddeley, CBE, FRS, FBA (1934-; F 1988-95) *Psychology*
Bryan Birch, FRS (1931-; F 1960-2) *Mathematics*
Alexander (Alec) Boksenberg, CBE, FRS (1936-; F 1996) *Astronomy*
Malcolm Bolton, FREng (1946-; F 1979-) *Engineering*
Sir Hermann Bondi, CBE, FRS (1919-2005; Master 1983-90, F 1990-2005) *Cosmology*
Donal Bradley, FRS (1962-; F 1989-93) *Physics*
Lord (Alec) Broers, FRS, FREng (1938-; Master 1990-6, F 1996-) *Microelectronics*
Sir Edward Bullard, FRS (1907-80; F 1960-80) *Geophysics*
Sir John Cockcroft, OM, CBE, FRS (1897-1967; Master, 1960-7) *Physics*
Francis Crick, OM, FRS (1916-2004; F 1960-2; Hon. Fell.) *Molecular biology*
William Dawes, FREng (1955-; F 1984-) *Engineering*
Nicholas Day, FRS, CBE (1939-; F 1986-92) *Epidemiology*
Robert Edwards, CBE, FRS (1925-; F 1979-) *Physiology*
David Epstein, FRS (1937-; F 1962-4) *Mathematics*
John Eshelby, FRS (1916-81; F 1965-6) *Materials science*
Douglas Gough, FRS (1941-; F 1972-) *Astrophysics*
Michael Gregory, CBE (1948-; F 1985-) *Manufacturing and management*
David Gubbins, FRS (1947-; F 1978-90) *Geophysics*
Sir John Gurdon, FRS (1933-; F 1973-95; Hon. Fell.) *Cell biology*
Sir William Hawthorne, CBE, FRS, FREng (1913-; Master 68-83, F 83-) *Engineering*
Antony Hewish, FRS (1924-; F 1961-) *Radio astronomy*
Archibald (Archie) Howie, CBE, FRS (1934-; F 1960-) *Physics*
Hugh Huxley, FRS (1924-; F 1966-87) *Molecular biology*
Alan Katrizky, FRS (1928-; F 1960-3) *Chemistry*
Anthony Kelly, CBE, FRS, FREng (1929-; F 1960-67, 1985-) *Materials science*
David Kendall, FRS (1918-2007; F 1962-2007) *Statistics*
Robert Kennicutt (1951-; F 2006-) *Astronomy*
Richard Keynes, CBE, FRS (1919-; F 1960-) *Physiology*
Julia King, CBE, FREng (1954-, F 1987-94, 2002-) *Engineering*
John Knott, FRS, FREng (1938-; F 1967-) *Metallurgy*
Simon Laughlin, FRS (1947-; F 1991-) *Neurobiology*

Early Fellows of Churchill captured in evocative 1960s photographs: Richard Adrian, physiologist; Sir Edward Bullard, geophysicist; Kenneth McQuillen, biochemist; Francis Crick, molecular biologist; Michael Young, sociologist; Andrew Sinclair, historian

Desmond McConnell, FRS (1930-; F 1962-88) *Crystallography*
Sir James Menter, FRS (1921-2006; F 1965-) *Metallurgy*
William Milne, FREng (1948-; F 1977-) *Engineering*
David Olive, FRS, CBE (1937-; F 1963-70) *Physics*
Stephen O'Rahilly, FRS, MD (1958-; F 1992-2006) *Clinical biochemistry*
Andrew Palmer, FRS, FREng (1938-; F 1967-75, 1996-) *Petroleum engineering*
John Pateman, FRS (1926-; F 1961-7) *Genetics*
Robert Ritchie, FREng (1948-; F 1972-4) *Materials science*
Carol Robinson, FRS (1956-; F 2003-) *Chemical biology*
Andrew Schofield, FRS, FREng (1930-; F 1963-6, 1974-) *Engineering*
Wolfram Schulz, FRS, MD (1944-; F 2004-) *Neuroscience*
Dennis Sciama, FRS (1925-99; F 1986-94) *Astrophysics*
Henning Sirringhaus, FRS (1965-; F 1999-) *Physics*
Franz Sondheimer, FRS (1926-81; F 1965-7) *Chemistry*
David Spiegelhalter, OBE, FRS (1953-; F 2007) *Statistics*
Christopher Strachey (1916-75; F 1962-5) *Computer science*
John Thompson, FRS (1932-; F 1968-) *Mathematics*
Janet Thornton, CBE, FRS (1949-; F 2002-) *Molecular biology*
David Thouless, FRS (1934-; F 1961-5) *Theoretical physics*
Sir David Wallace, CBE, FRS, FREng (1945-; Master 2006-) *Theoretical physics*
Simon White, FRS (1951-; F 1978-80, 91-4) *Astrophysics*
Peter Whittle, FRS (1927-; F 1967-) *Mathematics for Operational Research*
Dudley Williams, FRS (1937-; F 1964-) *Biological chemistry*
John Wood, CBE, FREng (1949- ; F 1974-8) *Engineering*
Peter Wroth, FEng (1929-91; F 1963-79) *Geotechnical engineering*

Some leading scholars in the humanities (excluding Overseas Fellows)
Includes all Fellows of the British Academy

Raymond Allchin, FBA (1923-; F 1963-) *Archaeology*
Sir Anthony (Tony) Atkinson, FBA (1944-; F 1992-4) *Economics*
Alan Baddeley, CBE, FRS, FBA (1934-; F 1988-95) *Psychology*
John Barnes, FBA, DSC (1918-; F 1969-) *Sociology*
Correlli (Bill) Barnett, CBE, DSC (1927-; F 1977-) *History*
Simon Blackburn, FBA (1944-; F 1967-70) *Philosophy*
Edward Craig, FBA (1942-; F 1966-) *Philosophy*
Martin Daunton, FBA (1949-; F 1997-2004) *History*
Sir Christopher Frayling (1946-; F 2009-) *Cultural history*
Frank Hahn, FBA (1925-; F 1960-) *Economics*
Oliver Hart, FBA (1948-; F 1975-81) *Economics*
Anthony Heath, FBA (1942-; F 1967-70) *Sociology*
Mary Jacobus, FBA (1944-; F 2000-) *English Literature*
John Killen, FBA (1937-; F 1961-9) *Classics*
Matthew Kramer, LLD (1959-; F 1994-) *Legal philosophy*
David Luscombe, FBA (1938; F 1964-70) *History*
Diarmaid MacCulloch, FBA, DD (1951-; F 1976-8) *History*
Sir Basil Markesinis, FBA, LLD (1944-; F 1970-4) *Law*
John Morrison, CBE, FBA (1913-2000; F 1960-65; Hon. Fell.) *Classics*
David Newbery, FBA (1943-; F 1966-) *Economics*
Richard Overy, FBA (1947-; F 1972-3) *History*
Jack Pole, FBA (1922-; F 1963-79) *History*

Roy Porter, FBA (1946-2002; F 1972-9) *History*
Captain Stephen Roskill, CBE, FBA (1903-82; F 1961-82) *Naval history*
Lord (Charles, 'C. P.') Snow, CBE (1905-80; F 1960-80) *Novelist*
George Steiner, FBA (1929-; F 1961-) *Comparative literature*
Sir Brian Vickers, FBA (1937-; F 1964-5) *English literature*
Derek Whiteside, FBA (1932-2008; F 1970-5) *History of science*
Sir Colin St John (Sandy) Wilson, RA (1922-2007; F 1960-72; Hon. Fell.) *Architecture*
Hugh Wood (1932-; F 1977-) *Composer*
Lord (Michael) Young, FBA (1915-2002; F 1961-6; Hon. Fell.) *Sociology*

Six buildings in Cambridge are named after Fellows: Broers Building, Bullard Laboratories, Cockcroft Lecture Theatre, Gurdon Institute, Schofield Centre, Michael Young Centre.

Appendix 6: Distinguished alumni
Includes all in Who's Who and some others besides; space permits only career snapshots.

Academic
Michael Ashburner, FRS (1942-): professor, Biology, Cambridge
Neil Ashcroft, FRS (1938-): professor, Physics, Cornell
Sir Anthony Atkinson, FBA (1944-): economist; Warden, Nuffield College, Oxford
James Binney (1950-): professor, Physics, Oxford
Sir Alan Budd (1937-): economist; Provost, Queen's College, Oxford
Mark Casson (1945-): professor, Economics, Reading
Justin Champion (1960-): professor, History, Royal Holloway, London
Christine Davies, OBE (1959-): professor, Physics, Glasgow
Roger Davies (1954-): professor, Astrophysics, Oxford
William Dawes (1955-): professor, Aeronautical Engineering, Cambridge
Stephen Dunnett (1950-): professor, Bioscience, Cardiff
Michael Green, FRS (1946-): professor, Theoretical Physics, Cambridge
Geoffrey Heal (1944-): professor, Public Policy, Columbia Business School
Howard Hodson, FREng (1957-): professor, Aerothermal Technology, Cambridge
Colin Humphreys, CBE, FREng (1941-): professor, Materials Science, Cambridge
Christopher Hunter, FRS (1965-): professor, Chemistry, Sheffield
Timothy Ingold (1948-): professor, Anthropology, Aberdeen
John Landers (1952-): Principal, Hertford College, Oxford
Diarmaid MacCulloch, FBA (1951-): professor, Church History, Oxford
Christopher Marshall, FRS (1949-): Director, Centre for Cell and Molecular Biology
John Marshall (1961-): professor, History, Johns Hopkins
Benjamin Martin (1952-): professor, Science Policy Studies, Sussex
Njabulo Ndebele, Hon. D.Litt. (1948-): author; Vice-Chancellor, Cape Town
David Otley (1944-): professor, Accounting and Management, Lancaster
Michael Pilling, CBE (1942-): professor, Physical Chemistry, Leeds
David Potts, FREng (1952-): professor, Soil Mechanics, Imperial
(Thomas) Maurice Rice, FRS (1939-): professor, Physics, Zurich
Brian Ripley, FRSE (1952-): professor, Applied Statistics, Oxford
Carol Robinson (1956-): professor, Biological Chemistry, Cambridge
Ian Roxburgh (1939-): professor, Astronomy, Queen Mary, London
Michael Rycroft (1938-): professor, International Space University, France
Lu Jeu Sham (1938-): professor, Physics, San Diego
Richard Smith, FBA (1949-): professor, Econometric Theory, Cambridge

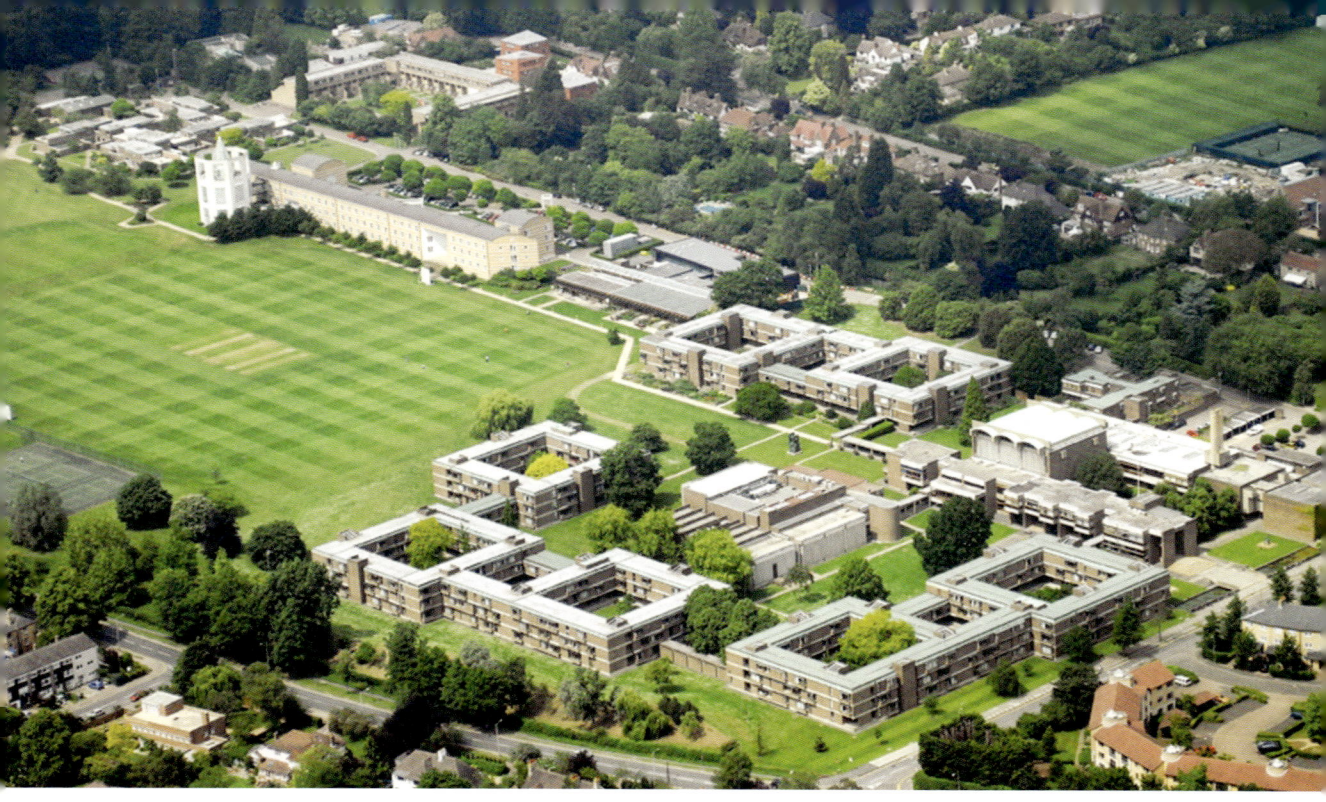

Churchill College from the air, looking north

Ian Stewart, FRS (1945-): professor, Mathematics, Warwick; science fiction author
Bjarne Stroustrup (1950-): computer scientist; inventor of C++
Fabian Tassano (1963-): libertarian economist and author
Geoffrey Thomas (1941-): President, Kellogg College, Oxford
Roger Tsien (1952-): professor, biochemistry, San Diego; Nobel Laureate
Neil Turok (1958-): Director, Institute of Theoretical Physics, Canada
Peter Wadhams (1948-): professor, Ocean Physics, Cambridge,

Arts, Media, Culture
Kari Blackburn (1954-2007): journalist, radio executive; Head of BBC Africa Service
Nicholas (Nick) Bryant (1986-): journalist; BBC Correspondent, Australia
Michael Copley (1956-): flautist; of the duo the Cambridge Buskers
Spencer de Grey, CBE (1944-): architect, Norman Foster and Partners
John Dunbar (1945-): artist, collector; founded Indica Gallery
Andrew Eaton (1959-): film producer; co-founder, Revolution Films
Peter Fincham (1956-): Director of Television, ITV
Sir Christopher Frayling (1946-): Rector, Royal College of Art; Chair, Arts Council
Gabriel Gbadamosi (1961-): poet, playwright, critic, broadcaster
Richard Holmes, OBE, FBA (1945-): author, biographer
Michael Lewin (1942-): novelist, playwright; professor, Comparative Literature, Harvard
Elizabeth McKillop (1953-): Director of Collections, Victoria and Albert Museum
(Brian) Alan Mills (1964-): composer and pianist
Viscount (Christopher) Monckton (1952-): journalist; former Prime Ministerial adviser
Anne Morrison (1959-): Controller, Network Production, BBC
Alexandra (Alix) Pryde (1973-): Distribution Controller, BBC
Alan Riach (1957-): poet; professor, Scottish Literature, Glasgow

Jonathan Rugman (1965-): TV journalist, Channel 4
Christopher Stoddart (1950-): CEO, Attheraces plc; former MD, GMTV
Timothy Supple (1962-): theatre, film, and opera director
Andrew Thomson, Hon. D.Litt. (1942-): Chair, DC Thomson (newspapers, comics)
Geoffrey Travis (1952-): founder, Rough Trade Records
Rick Warden (1971-): film and TV actor, including 'Band of Brothers'
James Wilkinson (1941-): freelance journalist and broadcaster

Charities
Julian Filochowski, OBE (1947-): Director, Catholic Fund for Overseas Development
(Paul) Robert Fulton (1951-): Chair, Ducane Housing Association
Caroline Harper, OBE (1960-): CEO, Sight Savers
Lord (Colin) Low, CBE (1942-): Chair, Royal National Institute of Blind People

Civil Service, Policy Advisers
Mark Adams, OBE (1962-): media consultant; formerly Prime Minister's office
Sir Peter Gershon, CBE, FREng (1947-): CEO, Office of Government Commerce
George Dudman, CB (1916-84): Legal Adviser, Department of Education and Science
Bernard Herdan, CB (1947-): CEO, Passport Agency
Stephen Inglis (1952-): Director, National Institute of Biological Standards
(John) Paul McIntyre (1951-): Head, Energy Strategy, Department of Energy
William Stow, CMG (1948-): Director General, Strategy, Department of Environment
Henry Walsh (1939-): Deputy Chair, Building Societies Commission

Diplomatic Service
Stuart Brooks, CMG, OBE (1948-): Counsellor, Foreign Office
Robert Court (1958-): Deputy High Commissioner, Australia
Hugh Davies, CMG (1941-): Senior Representative, Sino-British Liaison, Hong Kong
Denis Keefe (1958-): Ambassador to Georgia
Matthew Rous (1964-): Consul General, Indonesia

Education
Robert Douglas, CBE (1948-): Chair, Surrey Learning and Skills Council
(Ian) Philip Evans, OBE (1948-): Head Master, Bedford School
Timothy Mead (1947-): Registrary, Cambridge University
(Robert) Giles Mercer (1949-): Headmaster, Stonyhurst College
Andrew Ramsay (1948-): CEO, Engineering Council
Christopher Ray (1951-): High Master, Manchester Grammar School

Finance and industry
Malcolm Brinded, CBE, FREng (1953-): Director, Exploration and Production, Shell
Michael Burrows (1963-): co-creator, Alta Vista internet search engine
Gordon Campbell, CBE, FREng (1946-): Chair, British Nuclear Fuels
Michael J. J. Cowan (1952-): Director, Silchester International Investors
David Dutton (1943-): founder, Pizzaland Restaurants; Director, Daily Mail
Michael Gascoyne (1963-): designer of Formula One cars
Timothy How (1950-): CEO, Majestic Wine
Timothy Ingram (1947-): CEO, Caledonia Investments
Ian McCredie, OBE (1950-): Head, Global Security, Shell
Christopher Mairs, FREng (1957-): Chief Technical Office, MetaSwitch
David Marshall, CBE (1943-): Director General, Society of British Aerospace Companies

Colin Matthews (1956-): CEO, British Airport Authority (BAA)
Brendan O'Neill (1948-): CEO, ICI
Sir John Stuttard (1945-): partner, PricewaterhouseCoopers; Lord Mayor of London 2006-7
Eric Tait, MBE (1945-): Director, PKF Chartered Accountants
Richard Wakeling (1946-): CEO, Johnson Matthey

Law
Sir Hugh Bennett, QC (1943-): High Court Judge
John Cavell (1947-): Circuit Judge
Leonard Goldstone, QC (1949-): Circuit Judge
John Higham, QC (1952-): Recorder
Richard Holwell (1946-): Judge, Southern District, New York State
Clive Lewis, QC (1960-): Recorder
Gillian Morris (1953-): barrister; professor, Law, Brunel
Diana Parker (1957-): Senior Partner, Withers
Sir Philip Sales, QC (1962-): High Court Judge; formerly Treasury Counsel
David Stokes, QC (1944-2004): Judge, Central Criminal Court
Steven Whitaker (1950-): Senior Master, Supreme Court, Queen's Bench
Maha Zaki Yamani (1958-): first woman lawyer in Saudi Arabia

Medicine
Keith Barnett, OBE (1929-2009): Director, Centre for Small Animal Studies, Newmarket
John Deanfield (1952-): professor, Cardiology, University College, London
Paul Emery (1952-): professor, Rheumatology, Leeds
Paul Farrell (1953-): professor, Tumor Virology, Imperial College, London
Susan Lim (1955-): first surgeon to perform a liver transplant in Asia
Angus MacKay, OBE (1943-): Director, Mental Health, Lomond and Argyll
David Mant (1949-): professor, General Practice, Oxford
John Neoptolemos (1951-): professor, Cancer Studies, Liverpool
Sunitha Wickramasinghe (1941-): professor, Haematology, Imperial College, London
Robert Woods (1952-): professor, Clinical Psychology, Bangor

Military, Police
Rear-Admiral Timothy Chittenden (1951-): Chief of Staff to C.-in-C., Fleet
Air Vice-Marshall David Couzens (1949-): Director General, Defence Logistics, RAF
Robin Field-Smith, MBE (1948-): HM Inspector of Constabulary
Air Vice-Marshall Antony Nicholson, CBE (1946-): RAF
Admiral Donald Pilling (1943-2008): Vice-Chief, US Navy
Rear-Admiral Frederick Scourse, CB, MBE, FREng (1944-): Director General, Surface Weapons

Politics
HRH Prince Faisal Al Saud (1942-): Saudi Arabian royal family
Roger Helmer (1944-): Conservative Member of the European Parliament
Frank Maine (1937-): Liberal MP, Canada
Simeon Nyachae (1932-): government minister, Presidential candidate, Kenya
Karel Pinxten (1952-): Agriculture Minister, Belgium
Rt Hon. Gavin Strang, PC (1943-): Labour MP; former Minister of Transport
John Wilkinson (1940-): Conservative MP

Religion
Rt Rev. John Gladwin (1942-): Bishop of Chelmsford
Ven. Norman Russell (1943-): Archdeacon of Berkshire

Appendix 7: Principal benefactors

Founding appeal, 1958: *gifts of £35,000+ (today's equivalent: £500,000+)*

Associated Electrical Industries	Babcock and Wilcox (engineering)
Bowater Paper Corporation	British Motor Corporation
British Petroleum	Courtaulds (fibre manufacture)
Dorman Long & Co. (steel)	Dunlop Rubber Co.
English Electric	Esso Petroleum
Ford Foundation	Ford Motor Co.
General Electric	Gillette Industries
George Wimpey (construction)	Guest, Keen & Nettlefold (engineering)
Gulbenkian Foundation	Imperial Chemical Industries
Joseph Lucas (auto components)	Plessey Co. (electronics)
Portland Cement	Rockefeller Foundation
Rolls Royce (jet engines)	Shell Petroleum
Steel Company of Wales	Stewarts and Lloyds (engineering)
Transport and General Workers Union	Tube Investments (engineering)
Unilever (foodstuffs)	United Steel Companies
Vickers (engineering)	Garfield Weston Foundation (foods)
Winston Churchill Memorial Trust	Isaac Wolfson Foundation
F. W. Woolworth & Co. (retail)	

1985 appeal: *gifts of £50,000+ (today's equivalent: £500,000+)*

BASF (chemicals)	Dee Corporation (retail)
Shell Petroleum	

Since 1985: *gifts of £100,000+*

Hon. Walter Annenberg	Annenberg Foundation
Atlantic Philanthropies	Prince Bandar bin Sultan
Bill Brown Trust	British Petroleum
Winston Churchill Foundation of the United States	Clore Duffield Foundation
Douglas Daft Foundation	Mr John Duffield
Evergreen Group	Sir Paul Getty
Mrs Kyoko Gledhill	Mr Hamid Jafar
Hobson Charity	Mr Eric Hotung, CBE
Jupiter Asset Management	Sir Ka-shing Li
Møller Foundation	Andrew Mellon Foundation
National Heritage Lottery Fund	Mr David W. Packard
Royal Automobile Club	Raymond & Beverly Sackler Foundation
Mr Wafic Rida Said	Bernard Sunley Foundation
Margaret Thatcher Foundation	Mr Richard Tizard
Wing Yip Foundation	Garfield Weston Foundation
Dr Anthony H. Wild	Winton Foundation
Wolfson Foundation	Charles Wolfson Charitable Trust

Appendix 8: Buildings and architects

The original College (1960-68)	Richard Sheppard, Robson, and Partners
Wolfson Flats (1965-7)	David Roberts
Chapel (1966-7)	Richard Sheppard, Robson, and Partners

Archives Centre (1971-3)	Richard Sheppard, Robson, and Partners
Music Rooms (1979-80)	Richard Sheppard, Robson, and Partners
Møller Centre (1991-2)	Henning Larsen
Study Centre (1992-3)	David Thurlow, Carnell, and Thornburrow
Archives Centre Extension (2001-2)	David Thurlow, Carnell, and Curtis
Bondi, Broers, and Hawthorne Houses (2001-3)	Cottrell and Vermeulen
New Study & Music Centre (2006-7)	DSDHA (Deborah Saunt and David Hills)

Appendix 9: Arms, motto, colours, grace, declaration

The College arms, granted in 1959, are those of the Spencer-Churchill family, without supporters and with two modifications: the inclusion of an open book in both shield and crest. The heraldic description is: *Quarterly: 1 and 4, Sable, a lion rampant argent, on a canton of the last a cross gules; 2 and 3, Quarterly argent and gules, in the second and third quarters a fret or, on a bend sable three escallops also argent; over all in the fess point an open book likewise argent.* And of the crest: *On a wreath of the colours, a lion couchant gardant argent supporting with the dexter forepaw a staff or, flying therefrom a banner gules charged with an open book also argent.* The arms may be seen on the plaque outside the Porters' Lodge. Sir Winston's family arms are on the Colville Hall door. The grant of arms was funded by H. H. Corson, of Nashville, Tennessee.

The College motto is the single word, 'Forward'. This abridges 'Let us go forward together', the final phrase in Churchill's 'Blood, Toil, Tears and Sweat' speech, 13 May 1940, his first speech as Prime Minister, when Britain faced the German onslaught and France was on the verge of collapse. The phrase was popularised in a David Low cartoon, showing every class of Briton, sleeves rolled up, marching forward together. In 1945 the socialist *Daily Mirror* cleverly helped shift voters from wartime Churchillianism toward peacetime Labour government with the slogan, 'Forward with the People'.

The College colours are an unprepossessing chocolate and pink, Sir Winston's racing colours, registered with the Jockey Club, 1949, when he took up a new hobby. They had been his father's, Lord Randolph's, colours.

Despite Churchill being a secular college, grace is said at dinner, usually brief: *Benedictus benedicat* ('May the Blessed One give a blessing'), and, at dinner's end, *Benedicto benedicatur* ('Let a blessing be given by the Blessed One'). On formal occasions there is a longer grace: *Benedic, Domine, nos et dona tua, quae de largitate tua sumus sumpturi, et concede, ut illis salubriter nutriti, tibi debitum obsequium praestare valeamus, per Christum Dominum nostrum* ('Bless, O Lord, us and thy gifts, which from your bounty we are about to receive; and grant that, healthfully nourished by them, we may render you due obedience, through Christ our Lord.') At formal dinners there are two toasts, 'The Queen' and 'Sir Winston'.

At admission, Fellows make a declaration: 'I, [name], elected a Fellow of Churchill College, do solemnly declare that I will, so far as in me lies, loyally observe the Statutes, Ordinances, and customs of the College and in all things endeavour to promote learning and advance knowledge'.

Appendix 10: Roskill memorial lecturers
Established in memory of Captain Stephen Roskill, naval historian.

1985	Lord (Peter) Carrington, Secretary General of NATO
1987	Professor Sir Michael Howard, University of Oxford
1989	Field Marshal Lord (Michael) Carver, former Chief of Defence Staff
1991	Sir Brian Urquhart, former Deputy Secretary-General, United Nations
1993	Admiral of the Fleet Sir Julian Oswald, First Sea Lord
1995	Mr Mark Tully, Chief of Bureau, BBC, Delhi
1997	Professor Paul Kennedy, Director, International Security Studies, Yale

The Archives Centre, library and dining hall

1999	Sir Colin McColl, former Head of MI6
2001	Professor Peter Hennessy, Queen Mary, University of London
2003	Bridget Kendall, Diplomatic Correspondent, BBC
2005	HRH Prince Hassan bin Talal, former Crown Prince of Jordan
2007	Lord (Robert) May, former President of the Royal Society
2010	Mr Ken Livingstone, former Mayor of London

Appendix 11: Archives Centre: principal collections

Politics, diplomacy, and government
Leopold Amery (1873-1955), Secretary of State for India
Ernest Bevin (1881-1951), Labour Foreign Secretary
Reginald Brett, Lord Esher (1852-1930), Committee for Imperial Defence
Sir Alexander Cadogan (1885-1968), diplomat
Sir Winston Churchill (1874-1965), Conservative Prime Minister
Alfred Duff Cooper, Lord Norwich (1890-1954), Conservative First Lord of the Admiralty
Maurice Hankey (1877-1963), Cabinet Secretary
Quintin Hogg, Lord Hailsham (1907-2001), Conservative Lord Chancellor
Sir Bernard Ingham (1932-), press secretary to Prime Minister Thatcher
Neil Kinnock (1942-), Leader of the Labour Party
Sir Alan Lascelles (1887-1982), secretary to George VI and Elizabeth II
Selwyn Lloyd (1904-78), Conservative Foreign Secretary

Reginald McKenna (1863-1942), Liberal Home Secretary
David Maxwell Fyfe, Lord Kilmuir (1900-67), Conservative Home Secretary
Philip Noel-Baker (1889-1982), Labour Cabinet minister
Sir Eric Phipps (1875-1945), ambassador to Hitler's Germany
Enoch Powell (1912-98), Conservative Cabinet minister
Duncan Sandys (1908-87), Conservative Minister of Defence
Archibald Sinclair, Lord Thurso (1890-1970), Leader of the Liberal Party
Christopher Soames (1920-87), Conservative Cabinet minister
Margaret Thatcher (1925-), Conservative Prime Minister

Military
Admiral Sir John De Robeck (1862-1928), Dardanelles naval commander
Admiral John (Jackie) Fisher (1841-1920), naval commander, First World War
General Sir Ian Jacob (1899-1993), military secretary to the War Cabinet
Admiral Sir Bertram Ramsay (1883-1945), director of the Dunkirk evacuation
Field Marshal William Slim (1891-1970), commander, Burma
General Sir Louis Spears (1886-1974), head of mission to General de Gaulle

Science and technology
Sir Ove Arup (1895-1988), engineer and architect
Francis Bacon (1904-92), engineer
Sir Hermann Bondi (1919-2005), mathematician and cosmologist
Max Born (1882-1970), physicist
Sir Edward Bullard (1907-80), geophysicist
Sir James Chadwick (1891-1974), nuclear physicist
Sir John Cockcroft (1897-1967), nuclear physicist
Rosalind Franklin (1920-58), crystallographer
Sir William Hawthorne (1913-), aeronautical engineer
Archibald (A.V.) Hill (1886-1977), physiologist
Reginald (R.V.) Jones (1911-98), physicist, director of scientific intelligence
Richard Keynes (1919-), physiologist
Lise Meitner (1878-1968), nuclear physicist
César Milstein (1927-2002), molecular biologist
Max Perutz (1914-2002), molecular biologist
Sir Joseph Rotblat (1908-2005), physicist, founder of Pugwash
Sir Martin Ryle (1918-84), radio astronomer
Lord (Alexander) Todd (1907-97), chemist
Sir Frank Whittle (1907-96), inventor of the jet engine

Humanities
Captain Stephen Roskill (1903-82), naval historian
Lord (Michael) Young (1915-2002), sociologist, educationist

Churchill College
Cambridge
CB3 0DS

www.chu.cam.ac.uk

ISBN 978-0-9563917-1-1

9 780956 391711